W9-DFV-014

Mr. Robert Hoffman
10887 McDowell Rd.

The Official CRUISE Ship Joke Book

Introduction by Elliot Maxx

A special thanks to all the people who helped with this book,
my family, my wonderful wife, Laura, my kids and all the people
who shared so many great jokes over the years.

THE OFFICIAL CRUISE SHIP JOKE BOOK
Copyright 2004 by Elliot Maxx
Published by Fiasco Productions
ISBN # 0-935735-01-1

All rights reserved, including the right to reproduce this book or
portions thereof in any form.

CONTENTS

INTRODUCTION

I'm a comedian. I work on cruise ships. It's a pretty good job. There's no heavy lifting, and I can usually sleep in as late as I want. On a typical week, I might do two, maybe three shows. The rest of the time I hang out by the pool, play shuffleboard and go sightseeing in some of the most exotic locations in the world. And at the end of the week, they pay me.

Like I said, it's a pretty good job.

The best part of my job, though, is the people. I don't know what it is — maybe folks are just friendlier on vacation — but I've met some of the nicest people on cruise ships.

One of the things these people like to do, after a show, is come up and try out one of their favorite jokes on me.

They usually start by saying, "stop me if you heard this one," but I never do — not so much because I'm worried it might hurt their feelings (which it probably would) but mostly because a good joke is worth hearing more than once.

And I love a good joke.

Some people are picky about their jokes. Not me. I love all kinds. I love puns and one-liners and elephant jokes. I love dumb jokes. Like the one about the skeleton who walks into a bar and orders a beer and a mop. Or the bunnies who go on strike because they want a raise in celery.

I love the one about the two cannibals who are eating a clown and one says to the other, "Does this taste funny to you?"

I love the jokes you have to think about like, "Did you realize that half of all people are below average?"

Or "Why is 'abbreviation' such a long word?"

And I especially love those classic story jokes. Like the one about the newlyweds who are riding along in their buggy when their horse stops. So the guy gets down and looks at the horse and says, "That's one." And later, when the horse stops again, he says, "That's two." And when the horse stops a third time, he says, "That's three." And he pulls out a gun and shoots the horse dead. So his wife says, "What did you do that for, you stupid idiot? How are we going to get home now?" And the guy looks at her and says, "That's one."

One of the downsides to being a comedian is when people share a joke with you, they usually expect you to return the favor. Normally, this wouldn't be any big deal, but the truth is I'm not very good at telling jokes.

The problem is when I try to explain this, people think I'm kidding (that another downside to being a comedian -- people always think you're kidding) or perhaps I'm just being modest.

They assume, I must be a brilliant joke teller. I mean, isn't that what a comedian does for a living?

Well, technically it's not. Modern standup comedy isn't about jokes per se, at least not the "two guys walk into a bar" variety that we're talking about here. It's different. I can't say precisely what the difference is — but trust me, it's different.

It's like music. Opera is music. Willie Nelson does music. But do you really want to hear Willie Nelson doing opera?

I guess that's why I put this book together. Folks have been sharing their jokes with me for years and figured I owed them.

So I hope you enjoy reading this book. I know not everyone is going to laugh at every joke. I don't expect you to. People's senses of humor are like snowflakes — no two are alike.

Over the years, I've heard thousands of jokes from my fellow cruise ship travelers. Some funny and some not. What I tried to do in this book is maintain a PG rating and still include the funniest of the lot. So pick and choose what you like. And what you don't like, leave for somebody else.

The most important thing to remember is — laughter burns calories. And after a week on a cruise ship, that's a good thing.
Bon appetite!

Elliot Maxx
July 2004

GETTING THERE
IS HALF THE FUN

"Ladies and gentlemen, as we prepare for take off, please put your tray tables in their upright and locked position, and buckle your seatbelts.

"To buckle your seatbelt, remember: it works just like every other seatbelt, and if you don't know how to operate one, you probably shouldn't be out in public unsupervised.

"In the event of a sudden loss of cabin pressure, oxygen masks will drop from the ceiling. Stop screaming, grab the mask, and pull it over your face. If you are traveling with a child, or just a grownup acting one, secure your mask before assisting with theirs. If you are traveling with two children, decide now which one you love more.

"The weather at our destination is 70 degrees with some broken clouds, but we'll try to have them fixed before we arrive.

"Thank you and have a fabulous flight!"

A flamboyant flight attendant was checking to make sure everyone had their seatbelts fastened when he noticed a well-dressed, exotic-looking woman was still unbuckled.

"Excuse me dear," he said, politely, "Perhaps you didn't hear me, but we can't get going until you buckle your seatbelt. So if you could do that now, that would be just super."

The woman calmly turned her head and said, "In my country, I'm called a Princess. I take orders from no one."

"Well, lady," replied the flight attendant, "In my country, I'm called a Queen. So I outrank you — now buckle up!"

This guy was having a tough time lugging his lumpy, oversized travel bag onto the plane. The flight attendant had to help him stuff it in the overhead bin. When they finished, the stewardess said, "Do you always carry such heavy luggage?"

"Never again," said the man, mopping his brow. "Next time, I'm riding in the bag, and my wife can buy the ticket!"

A guy goes into a luggage store and says, "I'd like to get some straps for my suitcase."

The salesman asks, "How long do you need them?"

The guy says, "For quite awhile. We're going on a cruise."

A couple received two cruise ship tickets in the mail with a note that said, "Guess who sent these?"

Not wanting to look a gift horse in the mouth, they went on the cruise and had a great time. When they returned, they found their house had been burglarized. The only thing left was a note on the door that read, "Now you know."

On the day Bill and his wife, Eileen, were supposed to embark on their first cruise, Bill was called into work at the last minute. So he sent Eileen to the ship to get settled in with the intention of meeting up with her after work.

When he finally finished up at the office, Bill found himself racing through some unusually precarious rush hour traffic.

Eileen called him on his cell phone and said, "Bill, you better hurry. The ship is getting ready to set sail without you."

"I'm going as fast as I can," he said, "but traffic is terrible."

"Yes, I heard," said Eileen. "The news said there's some nut on the freeway driving the wrong way."

"One nut?" said Bill. "There must be hundreds of them!"

While packing for his first cruise, this guy says to his wife, "This is my emergency kit in case I get lost at sea. It's got flares, a radio and a deck of cards."

His wife asks, "What are the cards for?"

He says, "If the flares and radio don't work, I can take out the cards and play solitaire. In no time at all, someone will tap me on the shoulder and say, 'Put the red nine on the black ten.'"

This blonde sees a flyer advertising an ocean cruise for only five dollars. She goes to the address on the flyer and hands the secretary a five dollar bill. The secretary nods to a burly guy in the corner who walks over and knocks the blonde unconscious.

She wakes up to find herself tied up in the hold of a tramp steamer with a dozen others who've also been shanghaied.

She turns to the woman next to her and says, "Do you think they'll be serving food on this trip?"

At the Miami airport, a tourist forgot one of his bags in his car, so he went back to get it. When he got there, he saw a thief breaking into his trunk.

"Hey! That's my car!" he yelled.

"Okay," said the thief, "you take the radio. I'll take the tires."

TRAVEL BROCHURE DESCRIPTIONS AND WHAT THEY REALLY MEAN

TROPICAL	RAINY
GENTLE BREEZES	GALE FORCE WINDS
OLD WORLD CHARM	NO BATH
MAJESTIC SETTING	A LONG WAY FROM TOWN
OPTIONS GALORE	NOTHING IS INCLUDED
SECLUDED HIDEAWAY	IMPOSSIBLE TO FIND
EXPLORE ON YOUR OWN	PAY FOR IT YOURSELF
NO EXTRA FEES	NO EXTRAS, PERIOD.
NOMINAL FEE	OUTRAGEOUS CHARGE
COZY	SMALL
STANDARD	SUBSTANDARD
DELUXE	STANDARD
ALL THE AMENITIES	FREE SHOWERCAP
PLUSH	TOP AND BOTTOM SHEETS
LIGHT AND AIRY	NO AIR CONDITIONING
PICTURESQUE	THEME PARK NEARBY
OPEN BAR	FREE ICE CUBES
CONCIERGE	TOURIST BROCHURES
CONTINENTAL BREAKFAST	FREE MUFFIN

A elderly couple went to a vacation time-share presentation. As the salesman went into his close, he said, "And there are a ton of different activities for you and your spouse to participate in. What kind of things do you like to do on weekends?"

"Well," said the little old lady, "mostly we like to go around and listen to time-share presentations."

What do you get when you use LSD with birth control pills?

A trip without the kids.

Looking to book a cheap cruise on the internet, Lance and Sheila see an advertisement for a fourteen-day cruise at the astonishing price of only $199 per person.

When they arrive at the pier, they are surprised to find an exact replica of an ancient Roman galleon. Even the stewards and deckhands are dressed in ancient Roman garb.

As the gangplank is lifted, their steward leads them down a stairwell to the bottom of the ship, where they are chained along with dozens of other couples, and are forced to row to the rhythm of an enormous kettledrum played by a ferocious armored guard.

Whenever anyone slows down, they are whipped by another centurion who walks up and down the aisles.

They row like this for the next two weeks, receiving only meager rations of bread and water.

Finally at the end of the fourteenth day, they arrive back in Fort Lauderdale. As they stagger back to their rooms to pick up their luggage, Lance turns to Sheila and whispers, "By the way, how much are we supposed to tip the drummer?"

This guy is flying for the first time and he's a little nervous. He stops the stewardess walking up the aisle and says, "I hear the altitude can be pretty rough on your ears."

"That's true," says the stewardess, handing him a stick of gum, "but this usually does the trick."

After the flight, she sees the guy in the terminal and says, "Hey, did my suggestion help with the altitude?"

"It sure did," he says, "but I do have a question?"

"What's that?"

"How do I get the gum out of my ears?"

Old pilots never die.
They just go to a higher plane.

On the flight to Miami, the captain turns on the intercom to announce the plane will be arriving soon. When he finishes his announcement, he forgets to turn off the microphone.

Over the plane's intercom, the passengers hear the copilot say, "What are you going to do when we land?"

"Well," replies the captain, "First I'm going to have a nice cup of tea. Then I'm going to take that cute little blonde stewardess out to dinner and drinks, and then take her back to my place and make mad passionate love to her."

In the back of the plane, the poor stewardess' face turns bright red. As she runs up the aisle toward the cockpit, she trips over a little old lady's purse and sprawls on the floor.

As she's dusting herself off, the little old lady leans over to her and says, "No need to rush, dearie. He said he's going to have a cup of tea first."

A fellow goes up to the airlines ticket counter and says to the agent, "I'd like to purchase a ticket to Miami. However, I'd like to have my luggage sent to Seattle."

"I'm sorry, sir, but we can't do that."

"Why not? You did it last time."

This guy was sitting on a flight next to a woman who was nursing her baby. Noticing his discomfort, the woman turned to him and explained, "It helps to equalize the pressure in the baby's ears during take off."

"Really?" said the flustered man, "and to think all this time I've been chewing gum."

"If the black box is made to survive a plane crash, why don't they make the whole plane out of the stuff?"

A guy goes to a luggage store to do some window shopping. As he's leaving, the salesman says, "If you buy one today, we're offering a fifty dollar trade-in allowance on your old bag."

The guy thinks it over for a minute. Then he says, "I don't think so — I promised 'for better or worse.'"

A couple showed up at the airport just in time to see their plane taking off. The husband turned to his wife and said, "If you hadn't taken so much time getting ready, we wouldn't have missed our flight."

The wife said, "And if you hadn't been in such a big rush, we wouldn't have to wait so long for the next one."

On the way to the airport, this couple saw a sign that read, "Airport Left," so they turned around and went home.

A travel agent looked up from his desk to see an older lady and an older gentleman peering in the shop window at all the posters advertising glamorous destinations around the world.

The agent had had a good year and the sweet couple looking in the window gave him a rare feeling of generosity.

He invited them into his shop and said, "I know you are probably on a fixed income and could never hope to afford a vacation like one of these, so I've decided to send you off on a fabulous cruise at my expense."

When they tried to object, he interrupted and said, "I'm sorry, but I won't take no for an answer."

He booked two first class airfares and a stateroom on a five star cruise and sent them on their way.

About a month later, the little old lady came back to his shop.

"How did you like your vacation?" he asked eagerly.

"The flight was nice and the cruise was lovely," she said, "but one thing puzzles me."

"Really? What's that?"

"Who was that old guy I had to share the room with?"

WELCOME ABOARD!

This guy is walking through the terminal on embarkation day. He's got a suitcase in one hand and a poodle in the other.

A woman stops him and says, "I don't know if you know this, but they don't allow pets on the cruise ship."

It's too late to find someone to take care of his dog, so the guy decides to try and sneak him onboard. He puts on a pair of dark sunglasses. Then he puts a leash on the dog and starts to walk him up the gangway.

The security officer stops the guy and says, "Sir, I'm afraid we don't allow pets onboard."

"That's okay," says the guy. "This isn't a pet. This is my seeing-eye dog."

"You've got to be kidding," says the security officer. "You have a poodle for a seeing-eye dog?"

The guy says, "They gave me a poodle?"

A young couple planned to go on a Caribbean cruise together but the wife ran into some problems at work and had to join her husband a day late.

The first night onboard, the husband decided to email his wife to let her know how things were going. However, he mistyped her email address, accidentally sending the message to an elderly preacher's wife whose husband died just the day before.

When the grieving widow opened her email, she was horrified to read:

DEAREST WIFE,

I JUST CHECKED IN AND EVERYTHING IS READY FOR YOUR ARRIVAL TOMORROW.

YOUR LOVING HUSBAND

PS: IT SURE IS HOT DOWN HERE

The first day of the cruise, this lady uses the restroom in her cabin. She doesn't see the sign above the toilet warning not to flush while seated, and she ends up getting stuck.

She calls out to her husband, "I'm stuck. Do something."

Her husband tries to pry her loose, but he can't. So he calls the Purser's Desk and asks them to send help.

When he returns to the bathroom and explains the situation to his wife, she says, "I don't want some stranger to see me like this. Get me something to cover myself."

He takes off his hat and gives it to her to put on her lap.

A few minutes later there's a knock at the door. The plumber comes in, looks things over, and then says to the husband, "The good news is — I can help the lady. The bad news is — that fellow with the hat is a goner."

The hostess is checking tickets at the head of the gangway when a man opens his coat and exposes himself.

The hostess looks at him and says, "I'm sorry sir. I need to see your ticket, not your stub."

A young couple is joining the ship for their honeymoon. The blushing bride is a bit embarrassed to be known as a honeymooner, so when they get to the gangway, she asks her husband if there is any way they can make it appear as if they have been married a long time.

Her husband thinks for a moment and says, "Sure. You carry the luggage."

There was a mix-up with a woman's room. When she went to the front desk to remedy the situation, the purser asked, "Would you like an inside cabin or an outside cabin?"

She replied, "Well, it looks like it might rain today. I'd better get an inside cabin."

Did you hear about the passenger who put pizza in his wall safe and then called the front desk to complain his microwave wasn't working?

After seeing their cabin, this newlywed couple stormed down to the purser's desk to complain. The bride was in tears, and the groom was furious.

When asked what the problem was, the groom said, "I can't believe it. We booked a cabin with an ocean view and all we can see out our window is the parking lot

On embarkation day, the cabin steward was helping a frustrated passenger to his suite.

"What a day!" said the passenger. "I woke up this morning. I put on my shirt. A button fell off. I opened the dresser. The knob fell off. I picked up my suitcase. The handle fell off. I'm afraid to go to the bathroom!"

THE TOP TEN DUMB QUESTIONS ACTUALLY ASKED BY PASSENGERS

Does this elevator go to the front of the ship?

These photographs aren't marked – how will we know which ones are ours?

Does the ship generate its own electricity?

What do you do with the ice scuptures after they melt?

What time is the midnight buffet?

If I go snorkeling, will I get wet?

What floor is Deck 5 on?

How far are we above sea level?

Does the crew sleep onboard?

Has this ship ever sunk?

A lady called the front desk and said, "I'm trapped in my cabin. I can't get out."

"Have you tried the door?" asked the purser.

"Yes," said the lady, "but the one on the right led to the bathroom and the one on the left led to the closet."

"What about the door in the middle?" asked the purser. "Did you try that?"

"I would have," said the lady, "but it said, 'Do Not Disturb.'"

I'm not saying this passenger was dumb, but on the bottom of the embarkation form where it said, "Sign Here," the guy wrote, "Capricorn."

A woman was taking her first cruise. As she boarded the ship, she was very excited. The ship was grand and elegant. When she got onboard, everything was perfect: champagne, caviar, and a string quartet playing classical music.

Her impeccably dressed cabin steward greeted her in the lobby and took her bags.

"May I show you to your room?" he offered.

She followed him down a series of long corridors till they came to a set of beautiful brass doors. When the doors opened, she stepped inside and her face fell.

"I can't believe it!" she said. "Look at this room! It's so small! There's no window! There's no room for my luggage! There's not even a bed! Do you really expect me to stay in a dinky little room like this?"

"Of course not, madam," replied the cabin steward. "This is the elevator."

A snooty couple were taking their first cruise. The staff bent over backwards to make their trip a wonderful experience, but they complained about everything. The cabin was too small, the food was terrible, and the entertainment was just awful.

In an effort to make amends, the Hotel Director invited the couple to dine at the Captain's table.

When they received the invitation, the husband replied, "You must be joking! I didn't pay $5000 to eat with help!"

"Why is it called 'Tourist Season' if we can't shoot them?"

What's the difference between a crabby passenger and a puppy?
Eventually the puppy stops whining.

What's the definition of the Ship's Purser?
Someone who used to think he liked people.

"For every action there is an equal and opposite criticism."

A lady went to the purser's desk to complain about her bill, "My husband and I ordered a bottle of wine last night and you overcharged us for it."

"Ah yes," said the purser, "however, I notice here that on the previous night, you ordered a bottle of wine that we didn't charge you for at all. I don't recall you complaining about that."

"Well, no," said the woman. "I'm willing to overlook an occasional error, but this is two in a row."

On his first night aboard ship, this guy woke up with an upset stomach. He called room service and ordered some crackers. When he looked at the charge slip, he was furious.

He called room service and raged, "I know I'm on a luxury cruise, but $11.50 for six crackers is ridiculous!"

"Sir, the crackers are complimentary," the voice at the other end explained. "I believe what you are complaining about is your room number."

One group of passengers complained so much that, by the end of the cruise, their waiter started coming to their table and asking, "Is anything alright?"

"My cabin was so small, I had to go outside to change my mind."

I can't believe how small some of these cabins are! The first day of the cruise, my cabin steward opened my door. He said, "This is your stateroom."

I said, "What state? Rhode Island?"

I was on a cheap cruise last summer. One day, the cabin steward knocked on my door and asked if he could clean up.

I said, "Yes."

He came in, took a shower and left.

Be careful of discount cruise lines. On one cruise, I called the guy at front desk and said, "I got a leak in my sink."

He said, "Go ahead."

TEN SIGNS YOU'RE ON A CHEAP CRUISE

The Grand Buffet is a Happy Meal.

You turn on your cabin lights
and the ship slows down.

The Christmas Cruise is in August.

The television in your cabin only
has two channels. On and off.

The champagne bar features Ripple.

The string quartet only has three people.

The crew is wearing their gang colors.

Instead of x-raying your luggage, the
security guard just holds it up to the light.

You look up cheap in the dictionary
and find a picture of your ship.

They have to take up a collection
for the Bingo winner.

SHIP
OF FOOLS

Julie, the activities coordinator, was trying to coax a sullen guest into some of the onboard activities, but she wasn't having much luck. She said, "We have Cash Jackpot Bingo this afternoon. A lot of people enjoy that."

"I tried that once," said the lady, "I didn't like it and I haven't tried it since."

"Well," said Julie, "then how about Wooden Horse Racing? Have you ever tried that?"

"Yeah, once, and I didn't like that either," replied the lady, "and I certainly don't want to try it again."

"How about putt-putt golf?" asked Julie.

"Look," snapped the lady. "Why don't you just leave me alone? I don't want to be here. I wouldn't even have taken this trip if my daughter hadn't talked me into it."

"Oh," said Julie. "Your only child, I presume?"

A fellow went on a cruise and arranged to have his mother stay at his house and take care of his cat. Just to be on the safe side, he asked his neighbor to look in on them from time to time to make sure everything was all right.

A few days later, he called to see how things were going.

His neighbor said, "Your cat died."

The guy was flabbergasted. He said, "Is that any way to break bad news? Don't you have any compassion? I'm on vacation. I'm having a good time. Couldn't you try to break the news to me a little more gently?"

His neighbor said, "I'm sorry. How should I do that?"

The guy said, "Well, you could start by saying the cat was on the roof. Then, maybe the next day, tell me the cat fell off the roof. Then, the next day, tell me you took the cat to the vet and the vet had to put the cat to sleep. Something like that."

"I'm sorry. I didn't know."

"Aw, don't worry about it. By the way, how's my mother?"

"Well .. she's on the roof."

A passenger walks into the ship's library and says, "I'd like a Pina Colada, please."

The librarian says, "Ma'am, this is a library."

"Oh, I'm sorry," she says. Then she leans in and whispers, "I'd like a Pina Colada, please."

A passenger went into the ship's library, looking for a steamy romance novel. She picked out a book called, "Girl To Grab," but was disappointed when it turned out to be Volume 17 of the Encyclopedia Britannica.

A little old lady was looking around before the art auction when a contemporary painting caught her eye.

"What on earth is that supposed to be?" she asked.

The art auctioneer said, "That, my dear lady, is supposed to be a mother and her child."

"Well then," snapped the little old lady, "why isn't it?"

How many art auctioneers does it take to screw in a light bulb?

"One ... do I hear two? ... how about three?"

The art auctioneer asked a lady in the front row, "What is your opinion of this painting?"

"It's worthless," she said.

"I know," he replied, "but I'd like to hear it, anyway."

I love the art auctioneers, "This next piece is valued at over $20,000. Why don't we start the bidding at say ... eight bucks."

The cruise director noticed they were out of ping pong balls on the sports deck, so he stopped by the storage area and put several in each of his pockets to replenish the supply.

On his way back, an elderly woman joined him in the elevator. Out of the corner of his eye, he noticed her staring down at the front of his pants.

Embarrassed by his peculiar appearance, he turned to her and explained, "Ping pong balls."

"I see," she said. "Well, if it's anything like tennis elbow, it must be very painful."

One night in the casino, the pit boss noticed this passenger hanging around the change machine.

The guy would go up to the machine and put in a twenty dollar bill. Then he would fill his bucket with quarters and take them back to the cashier's window where he'd trade them in for another twenty dollar bill. Then he would head back to the change machine and start over again.

Finally, the pit boss asked the guy, "How are you doing?"

The guy said, "Not too bad. So far, I'm about even."

An attractive young lady went over to the craps table late one night. She put $5000 down on the pass line and said to the dealers, "Rolling dice in the buff always brings me luck. Since there's no one else in the casino, do you mind?"

The two dealers looked at each other and readily agreed.

So the woman stripped off her clothes. Then she rolled the dice and yelled, "I won! I won!"

Then she scooped up the money, grabbed her clothes and left.

The two dealers stood there, dumbfounded.

"What did she roll anyway?" asked the first dealer.

"I don't know," said the second dealer. "I thought you were watching the dice."

This lady approached the Cruise Director one morning and said, "I was wondering if you have church services onboard?"

He said, "Yes, we do. As a matter of fact, we have church services every evening in the casino."

"Really?" she said. "What denomination?"

"Usually tens and twenties."

A woman had been sitting in the buffet most of the day when the Cruise Director came by and asked what she was up to.

The lady said, "I'm trying to put together this jigsaw puzzle but I can't seem to get any of the pieces to fit."

"What's the puzzle of?" he asked.

"It's a picture of a big rooster, but it's very hard," she said. "I can't seen to get any of the edge pieces to fit. Maybe you could you give me a hand?"

When the Cruise Director got next to her table, he saw her problem immediately. He said, "Ma'am, why don't we put the cornflakes back in the box and see if we can't find you something easier to work on?"

"Gold by the inch? Who needs an inch of gold?"

A boy and his father are out on the promenade deck one day. While they're walking along, the boy asks, "Dad, how does the ship stay afloat?"

His father says, "I don't really know, son."

A little while later, the boy asks, "Dad, how do the fish breathe underwater?"

His father says, "I don't really know, son."

A little while later, the boy asks, "Dad, why is the sky blue?"

His father says, "I don't really know that either, son."

A little while later, the boy looks up at his father and says, "Dad, do you mind me asking you all of these questions?"

His father says, "No, of course not, son. If you don't ask questions, how can you expect to learn anything."

This distinguished older gentleman sat in the same spot by the pool every day. It was fairly obvious from his Rolex watch and his diamond pinky ring that he was fabulously wealthy.

One day, this young fellow sat down next to him and asked how he made his money.

The old guy sat back and said, "Well, son, it was 1932. The depth of the Great Depression. I was down to my last nickel. I invested that nickel in an apple. I spent the entire day polishing that apple and at the end of the day, I sold it for ten cents.

"The next morning, I invested those ten cents in two apples. I spent the entire day polishing them and sold them at five o'clock for twenty cents. I continued this system and by the end of the month, I'd accumulated $1.37.

"Then my wife's father died and left us two million dollars."

The social hostess noticed a passenger sitting by himself, looking quite forlorn. She went over and asked him, "What seems to be the matter?"

"Well, since you asked," he said, "I'll tell you. Last June, my mother died and left me 20,000 dollars."

"I'm sorry to hear that."

"Then, in July," he continued, "my father passed away and left me 15,000 dollars."

"Oh, that's terrible."

"Then, last month," he said, "my uncle, Harry, died and left me 25,000 dollars."

"That must be devastating," she said, "losing three family members in three months."

"Yes," he said, "then, this month, nothing."

Two ladies are poolside, talking.   One says to the other, "I hear your son is seeing a psychiatrist."

"Yes."

"So, what's his problem?"

"His doctor says he has an Oedipus Complex."

"Oh, Oedipus-schmoedipus — as long as he loves his mother."

Two ladies are checking out the onboard activities listed in the Daily Program.

One says to the other, "They have transcendental meditation at four o'clock. You wanna try that?"

The other one says, "Why not? It's got to be better than just sitting around doing nothing."

Two other women are out sunning themselves by the pool. The first one says, "So I hear your son is going to college."

"That's right."

"What do you think he'll be when he gets out."

"Probably 35 or 40."

Three ladies are sitting on deck, talking about their children.

The first lady says, "My son, Irving, calls me every week, long distance! Such a wonderful boy, and he loves his mother!"

"You call that love?" says the second lady. "My son, Stanley, he loves me so much, he calls me twice a week and comes to dinner every Sunday! Now that's love!"

The third lady says, "That's nothing! My son, Barry, goes five days a week to see a psychoanalyst and what does he talk about? Me!"

One afternoon, a little boy accidentally swallowed a quarter and got it lodged in his throat. His mom was frantic. She didn't know what to do.

Fortunately, another passenger came by who said he could help. He turned the boy upside down and patted him on the back, dislodging the quarter.

"Thank you," said the mother. "I didn't know what to do?"

"No problem," said the guy. "I've had a lot of experience with this sort of thing."

"Really," said the mother. "Are you a doctor?"

"No, I work for the IRS."

An obnoxious little boy had been getting on everyone's nerves during the cruise. He would run into people on the stairs, push all the buttons in the elevator, draw on the pictures in the photo gallery and generally make a nuisance of himself.

One day, he ran up to the ship's security officer and cried, "I've lost my parents. Can you help me?"

As they looked around the ship for his parents, the little boy said, "Do you think we will ever find them?"

"It's hard to say," said the security officer. "There are so many places for them to hide."

A passenger went into the gift shop and asked if they had anything for hiccups. Without warning, the clerk slapped him in the face.

"What was that for?" asked the astonished passenger.

"Well," said the clerk, "you don't have the hiccups anymore."

"I never did," said the passenger. "It was my wife!"

This farmer is taking his first cruise. He is trying to impress the girls at the pool, but he's not having any luck.

So his buddy suggests, "Why don't you stuff a potato in your swim trunks? I bet that would impress the ladies."

So he gets a potato from the buffet, stuffs it in his trunks, and heads to the pool. When he returns, he's totally embarrassed, "That was a stupid idea! Everybody laughed at me! Look!"

His buddy takes a look and says, "Well, no wonder — the potato is supposed to go in the front!"

"Why is it the last person you want to see in a Speedo is always the one who's wearing one?"

One day at sea, a passenger is watching the waves in the pool. He asks a deckhand, "Is it filled with fresh water or sea water?"

"Sea water, I think."

"Well, that explains why it's so rough."

How do middle-aged men exercise on a cruise ship?

By sucking in their gut every time a bikini walks by.

Sally and her sister, Ruth, were sitting near the pool so they could keep an eye on their children.

At every turn, Sally was yelling at her son, "Benjamin, don't run! You'll slip and crack your skull open! Benjamin, you be careful! You could put your eye out with that thing! Benjamin, stay away from the deep end! You'll drown yourself!"

"My goodness! He sure is active," said Ruth.

"Yes," said Sally, "and such a nervous child."

The youth counselor was walking along the deck when he noticed an twelve-year-old kid sitting by the pool, sipping a Margarita and smoking a Cuban cigar.

The counselor walked up to him and said, "Excuse me, young man, are your parents around?"

The kid nonchalantly flicked the ash from his cigar and said, "What do you think?"

A young lady spent most of her cruise sunbathing on the top deck of the ship. She wore a bathing suit the first day. But on the second day, she decided that no one could see her way up there. So she slipped out of it to get an overall tan.

She'd hardly begun when she heard someone running up the stairs. Since she was lying on her stomach, she just pulled a towel over her rear end to cover herself.

A flustered deckhand ran up to her and said, "Excuse me, miss, the cruise line doesn't mind you sunbathing up here, but you are going to have to keep your bathing suit on."

"What's the difference?" asked the young lady. "No one can see me up here, and besides, I'm covered with a towel."

"Not exactly," said the embarrassed deckhand. "You're lying on the dining room skylight."

The Cruise Director was hosting a ship version of the popular game show, WHO WANTS TO BE A MILLIONAIR? He asked a contestant to spell the word 'fascinate' and use it in a sentence."

The passenger spelled the word correctly and then added, "Fascinate. I got a sweater with ten buttons on it, but after all the weight I've gained this trip, I can only fascinate."

A while later, the Cruise Director asked another contestant, "What is the capital of Michigan?"

"That's easy," replied the passenger, "it's 'M.'"

An old fellow was sitting by the pool one afternoon when this young guy sits down next to him and starts bragging about all of his accomplishments.

"I got a really nice place back home," he says. "I got this big house with a pool and I got so much land, I haven't even seen it all. You know, I can hop in my pickup, drive all day and still not get from one end to the other."

The old fellow nods and says, "Yeah, I used to have a truck like that."

A lady was looking through the brochure of the many exotic beauty treatments offered at the ship's spa when she saw they offered milk baths.

"What is a milk bath?" she asked the attendant.

"You soak in a tub full of warm milk," said the attendant. "It promotes a smoother, creamier complexion."

"Is is pasteurized?" she asked.

"No," said the attendant, "just up to your neck."

After an afternoon at the spa, this lady said to her husband, "The fitness counselor said I have a gorgeous body. I have the skin of a teenager and the figure of a twenty-five-year old."

Her husband said, "Oh yeah? Well, what did he say about your 65 year old ass?"

She said, "Your name never came up."

While passing the gym one day, one lady passenger said to her friend, "If God wanted us to bend over, He would have put diamonds on the floor."

Why did the aerobics instructor cross the road?
Because somebody on the other side could still walk.

> **"A cruise ship is the only place you can see people wait twenty minutes for the elevator so they can go up to the gym and use the stairmaster."**

The fitness instructor is talking with this guy in the gym. He says, "You're in great shape for a sixty-year-old man."
The guy says, "Who says I'm sixty?"
The instructor says, "I'm sorry. How old are you?"
The guy says, "I turn eighty-two next month."
"Eighty-two!" says the instructor. "Do you mind if I ask how old your dad was when he died?"
"Who says my father's dead?"
"He's not dead?"
"Nope, he'll be 103 this year."
"Amazing. How old was your grandfather when he died?"
"Who says my grandfather's dead?"
"He's not dead."
"He'll be 125 this year, and he's getting married next week."
"Wow! That's incredible! But why, at his age, would he want to get married?"
"Who says he wants to?"

This blind guy goes into the gift shop one afternoon. He takes his seeing eye dog by the leash and starts swinging him around over his head.

The shop manager says, "Can I help you?"

The guy says, "No thanks. I'm just looking around."

How do you get an 80 year old grandmother to say the f-word?

Get another 80 year old grandmother to say, "Bingo!"

The gift shop manager got a call from a drunken passenger in the middle of the night who wanted to know what time the shops would be opening.

The manager was furious. He slammed down the receiver and went back to bed. A few minutes later, the man called back.

"Sir," said the manager, "I can't believe you could be so inconsiderate as to wake me at this hour. The shops will be open in the morning and I will be glad to let you in then."

"Oh, I don't want to get in," said the drunken passenger. "I want to get out."

This lady booked her eleven-year-old son's ticket at a reduced rate. So before they boarded the ship, she took her son aside and said, "Remember, if anyone asks, you're still ten."

One afternoon, the Cruise Director struck up a conversation with the boy. They talked about school and sports and at one point, he asked the boy, "And how old are you, young man?"

The boy said, "I'm ten."

"Really, and when do you turn eleven?"

"As soon as we get off this ship."

Halfway through their cruise, this couple decides to call home and see how their teenage children are getting along. When their sixteen-year-old son answers the phone, the father asks, "How's everything going?"

"Oh, everything's going great, Dad, but I don't think we're going to be able to pick you and Mom up at the airport."

"Really? Why not?"

"Well, your car won't start."

"Why not?"

"I think there's water in the carburetor."

"Water in the carburetor?"

"Yeah, I'm pretty sure that's the problem."

"And how would you know that? You don't know the first thing about cars. Where's the car now?"

"In the swimming pool."

I CAN'T BELIEVE I ATE
THE WHOLE THING

A French guy calls room service, "I would like some pepper?"
"Black pepper or white pepper?"
"Toilet pepper."

The first day of the cruise, a waiter is explaining the dining room schedule to some new passengers. He says, "Breakfast is from seven to eleven. Lunch is from twelve to three, and supper is from six until eleven."

"You're kidding," said one of the passengers. "When are we ever going to find time to do any sightseeing?"

This passenger says to the waiter, "Could you bring me a hamburger without onions."

The waiter says, "I'm sorry, sir, we're out of onions. Perhaps I could bring it without pickles instead?"

A surly passenger goes into the dining room and snaps at the waiter, "Are you serving crabs, tonight?"

The waiter says, "Certainly sir, what would you like?"

A passenger called room service and ordered a pizza. The steward asked if he should cut it in six or twelve pieces.

"Better make it six pieces," said the passenger. "I don't think I could eat twelve."

How can you tell you've spent too much time at the buffet?

When the weatherman says, "It's chilly outside," and you run out the front door with a spoon.

What's a cruise ship passenger's idea of "eating light?"

As soon as it's light, they start eating.

During dinner one night, Saul says to his wife, "Sadie, I tink I svallowed a bone."

"Are you choking?"

"No, I'm serious."

An old guy goes up to the Cruise Director and says, "I want to complain about the waiters in the buffet."

The Cruise Director says, "I'm sorry to hear about that, sir. Our waiters pride themselves on their efficiency."

"That's the problem. They're too efficient. I put my lunch on the table. I go to get a glass of tea. I come back — my lunch is gone. I go to get more lunch. I come back — my tea is gone. I'm standing in a room full of food and I'm starving to death!"

YOU KNOW YOU'VE OVERDONE IT AT THE BUFFET WHEN ...

YOU CUT YOUR FINGER AND GRAVY POURS OUT.

YOU HAVE TO PULL DOWN YOUR
PANTS TO GET IN YOUR POCKETS.

YOUR PICTURE IN THE PHOTO GALLERY
SAYS, "CONTINUED ON OTHER SIDE."

YOU GO TO A RESTAURANT AND INSTEAD
OF A MENU, THEY GIVE YOU AN ESTIMATE.

YOU STEP ON A TALKING SCALE AND
IT SAYS, "ONE AT A TIME PLEASE."

YOU GET IN AN ELEVATOR
AND IT WILL ONLY GO DOWN.

YOU GET YOUR SHOES SHINED AND
HAVE TO TAKE THE GUY'S WORD FOR IT.

YOUR BEEPER GOES OFF AND
PEOPLE THINK YOU'RE BACKING UP.

YOU TRY TO GET OUT OF BED AND END UP
ROCKING YOURSELF BACK TO SLEEP.

YOU GO JOGGING AND SET OFF CAR ALARMS.

YOU FALL ASLEEP AT THE BEACH AND GREENPEACE
WORKERS TRY TO PUSH YOU BACK IN THE WATER.

A couple were sitting in the buffet one day. When the woman came back to the table with her fifth helping, her husband said, "That's the fifth time you've gone back for more food. Aren't you a little embarrassed? "

"No," she said. "I just tell them I'm getting it for you."

"Eat, drink and be merry For tomorrow we diet!"

A guy went into the dining room and sat with some other passengers. When the waitress came over and asked what he'd like, he announced, "I'd like a quickie."

She slapped his face and said, "Just give me your order, please."

He said, "I would like a quickie."

She slapped him again and said, "All right, this is your last chance. What do you want?"

The guy said, "I would really like a quickie,"

After she slapped him a third time and stormed off, the lady sitting next to him leaned over and said, "I believe it's pronounced quiche."

"If we're not supposed to eat animals, why are they made out of meat?"

On the first day of the cruise, a passenger was standing in the buffet line looking at the food. The chef walks up to him and says, "You know, two of the dishes I am most famous for are the Chicken Coq Au Vin and the Key Lime Pie."

"Really?" says the guy, "and which one is this?"

A passenger goes into the buffet. He asks the chef, "How do you prepare your chickens?"

"Nothing special," says the chef. "We just tell them straight out they're gonna die."

HAM AND EGGS:
A day's work for the chicken.
A lifetime commitment for the pig.

Why do seagulls fly over the sea?
  Because if they flew over the bay, they'd be bagels.

Why did the cookie visit the ship's doctor?
  Because he felt crummy.

What did one hot dog say to another?
  Hi, Frank.

What is bright orange and sounds like a parrot?
  A carrot.

Why was the tomato red?
  Because it saw the salad dressing.

What do you get when you eat beans and onions?
  Tear gas.

What's the difference between roast beef and pea soup?
  Anyone can roast beef.

A young couple from San Francisco were cruising with their precocious four-year old daughter, Jessica. Each night, in the dining room, they were seated with a rather staid, older couple who were not only boring, but insisted on saying a rather long winded prayer before each meal.

On the last night of the cruise, one of the older grownups suggested that perhaps little Jessica would like to have the honor of saying grace before dinner.

Embarrassed, Jessica whispered to her mother, "But, mom, I don't know how to say grace."

Her mother patted her head and said, "Just say what daddy said at breakfast, dear. You know, 'Oh God ...'"

"Oh God," said Jessica, bowing her head, "do we have to eat with those boring, old people again tonight?"

"I don't understand what it is about the ocean air — but you hang something in your closet for a week and it shrinks two sizes."

A lady was going through the buffet line, but she was having a difficult time with the exotic dishes.

"Caviar?" asked the server.

"Oh no," she said, "I couldn't eat anything that came out of a fish's stomach."

"Perhaps some sliced tongue?" he offered.

"No," she said, "I couldn't eat anything from a cow's mouth."

"Then what would you like, ma'am?" he asked.

"Oh, I don't know," she sighed. "Maybe I'll just have some scrambled eggs."

A lady asked the wine steward, "Do you prefer port or sherry?"

The wine steward said, "I would have to say the port. A glass of vintage port is almost orchestral in its complexity. Between the bouquet and the finish is such a mix of colors and textures, there is no comparison. And besides, sherry makes me fart."

"Life not only begins at forty, it begins to show."

A woman was watching her husband standing on the scale at the gym, sucking in his stomach.

Thinking he was using this maneuver to weigh less, she commented, "I don't think that's going to help."

"Sure it will," said her husband. "It's the only way I can see the numbers."

I gained so much weight on my last cruise that when I got home, I qualified for group insurance.

After a week onboard, one lady had put on more than just a few pounds. It was especially noticeable when she tried to squeeze into a pair of her old blue jeans.

Wondering if the added weight was noticeable to anyone else, she asked her husband, "Honey, do these jeans make me look like the broadside of the ship?"

"Not at all," he replied. "The ship isn't blue."

This lady goes to the gym. When she returns, she says to her husband, "Honey, I think I lost a few pounds."

"Well, turn around," he says. "I think I found them."

What's the difference between embarkation and debarkation?
  About ten pounds.

How can you spot an anorexic at a cruise ship buffet?
  No third helpings.

Returning home after a two-week cruise, this lady went to the doctor and asked for his advice on how to lose weight fast. He said, "Eat anything and everything you want for the first two days of your diet. Then skip the third day."

So she went home and ate anything and everything she wanted for the first two days and then skipped the third day.

The next day the doctor called and asked her how her new diet was going.

She said, "Well, the first two days were easy, but that third day was hard. I'm just exhausted from all that skipping."

"Brain cells come and go but fat cells live forever."

Two women are standing in line at the buffet. The first one says, "I never eat red meat, processed food, or anything with preservatives or chemicals in it."

"That's great," says the other. "How do you feel?"

"Hungry."

Two guys are talking in the gym. One says to the other, "Man, I can't believe how much weight I gained on this cruise! I can't even touch my toes!"

"Touch them?" says the other. "I'd be happy just to see them!"

An English gentleman is passing through the buffet line. He looks suspiciously into one of the pots and asks, "What is this?"

"It's bean soup," says the chef.

"I'm sure it has," says the Englishman, "but what is it now?"

This passenger was furious when his steak arrived too rare. He called the waiter over and said, "Didn't you hear me when I said, 'well done'?"

"Yes sir," replied the waiter, "And thank you very much. I always appreciate a compliment."

One night in the dining room, this snooty lady sits down and orders a glass of wine. When the waiter comes to take her dinner order, she glances at the menu and says, "I'll have the Guisseppe Spomadalucci."

"I'm sorry, ma'am," says the waiter, "but you've just ordered the chef."

This lady is standing on the scale in the gym. She says, "I can't believe it. I've been watching what I eat all cruise and this scale says I'm heavier than when we started — here, honey, hold my jacket. It still says I'm heavier — here, hold my donuts."

Did you hear about the new garlic diet?

You don't lose weight, but you look thinner from a distance.

Did you hear about the new Three Martini Diet?

It doesn't curb your appetite, but the food keeps falling out of your mouth.

How can you tell you've been on too many cruises?
    Your clothes have stretch marks.

A beggar approaches a passenger as she's leaving the ship.
He says, "Lady, I haven't eaten in days."
    She says, "If only I had your willpower."

What's the difference between a cruise ship passenger and a great
white shark?
    One is a highly evolved eating machine that devours every-
    thing in its path. The other is a fish.

THE BOOZE CRUISE

This guy is sitting in the lounge when the purser comes on the intercom and says, "Will Mister Harrison please pick up the white courtesy phone. We have a lost child at the front desk."

He gets up and starts for the door. Then he stops and thinks, "Wait a minute. What am I thinking? I don't have any kids."

A few minutes later, the intercom clicks on again, "Will Mister Harrison please report to the purser's desk. Your wife would like to speak with you."

The guy jumps up and heads for the door again. Then he stops and thinks, "Wait a second. I'm not married."

A few minutes later, the intercom clicks on again and he hears, "Will Mister Harrison please contact the ship's purser. We have an important message from your family."

The guys jumps up a third time and then he thinks, "Wait a minute. My name's not Harrison."

This guy and his wife go into the ship's lounge. The guy calls the bartender over and says, "You better give me a beer. It's going to start soon."

The guy's wife looks at him and says, "What's going to start?"

The guy says, "You'll see."

Then he drinks the beer and says to the bartender, "You better get me another. It's going to start soon."

His wife says, "What's going to start?"

He says, "You'll see."

Then he drinks the next beer and says to the bartender, "You better bring another. It's going to start soon."

His wife says, "That's your third beer in less than an hour. Don't you think you should slow down a little?"

The guy says, "And now it starts."

One night, the security officer sees a guy relieving himself on the promenade deck. He says, "Sir, you can't do that here."

The guy looks up and says, "You know, I was thinking the same thing — but when I tried to use the restroom upstairs, the sign said: Toilet Broken — Use deck below."

The waiter approached a rather crabby looking couple sitting in the lounge.

"Something from the bar?" he asked.

"I'll have a rum and Coke," said the wife.

"I'll have the same," snapped the husband. "But make sure I get a clean glass."

The waiter returns with their drinks and says, "That's two rum and Cokes and ... which one of you wanted the clean glass?"

Late one night, the ship's security officer noticed a drunken passenger sneaking down the hallway.

"What are you doing out this late?" asked the officer.

"I'm going to a lecture," said the man.

"Really?" said the security officer, "And just who's going to be giving a lecture at this hour?"

"My wife."

One night, a female guest was sitting in the ship's disco. She was obviously inebriated. Spotting her, the Cruise Director stopped and offered to escort her to her cabin, "Ma'am, it very late. Perhaps I should walk you home?"

"Ssschertainly," replied the drunken woman, with a wink. "But you might jussht have to carry me."

"My pleasure," he replied. "What cabin are you in?"

"I dunno," she slurred, "but when I shee it, I'll remember it."

So the Cruise Director hoisted her into his arms and proceeded to carry her through the corridors.

At one point, the drunken woman looked up into his eyes and whispered, "You're passionate."

"Why, thank you," he replied, and continued down the hall.

A little louder, the woman said, "You're passionate."

"Yes," he said, "Thank you very much."

"Your passionate!" she screamed.

"Madam, please," he said, "I don't have time for this kind of nonsense. We have rules against fraternizing with the guests and besides, I'm married. Let's just find your room."

"Thassh what I been trying to tell you!" she said, pointing behind him. "My room -- you're passhing it!"

A lady was walking on deck with her little boy when a drunken passenger staggered up to her and said, "Oh my god! That is the ugliest kid I've ever seen in my life!"

When he staggered off, the woman sat in a deck chair and burst into tears.

A waiter saw her crying. He walked over and said, "Excuse me, ma'am, but what is the matter?"

She said, "I've just been terribly insulted."

"I'm so sorry to hear that, ma'am," said the waiter. "Would you like a tissue to dry your eyes? And how about a banana for your little monkey?"

"Wine improves with age. The older I get, The more I like it."

One night, a passenger got so drunk he fell off his barstool and couldn't get back up. The bartender called security and had them send an officer to help the man back to his cabin.

The officer tried several times to help the man to his feet but he just slumped back to the floor.

He ended up having to drag the man back to his cabin. When they got there, the man's wife opened the door.

"What's going on here?" she asked.

"Your husband needed a little help getting back from the bar," said the security officer.

"Well, thank you," she said.

"No problem," replied the officer.

"Just one thing," she said. "Where's his wheelchair?"

On a ship, how can you tell which passengers are drunk?

They're the ones walking in a straight line.

After watching one of the passengers belting down drink after drink, the bartender said, "I think you've had enough."

"Aw, give me a break," said the drunken passenger. "I just lost my wife."

"Gosh, I'm sorry," said the bartender. "It must be hard losing your wife."

"Hard?" said the drunk. "It's darn near impossible."

A passenger goes into the lounge and says to the Chinese bartender, "Give me a Stoli with a twist."

The bartender thinks for a second. Then he smiles and says, "Okay ... once upon time there was four little peegs ..."

This guy is having a beer in one of the ship's lounges when he hears a soft voice say, "Nice shirt."

He looks around but the place is empty except for himself and the bartender.

A few minutes later, he hears, "Great tie."

He looks around. Again, nothing.

A little later, he hears, "Excellent haircut."

Finally, he calls the bartender over and says, "I must be losing my mind. I keep hearing voices saying nice things and there's not a soul in here except you and me."

"Don't worry," says the bartender. "It's the peanuts."

"Say what?"

"It's the peanuts. They're complimentary."

This guy is sitting in the bar all day, getting drunk. After awhile, he gets up to use the bathroom. He's in there for a few minutes and everything's fine. Then, all of a sudden, he starts yelling and screaming at the top of his lungs.

The bartender goes in to check on him, "Sir, what are you yelling about? You're scaring the other passengers."

The guy looks up and says, "When I tried to flush the toilet, something bit me on the rear end!"

The bartender says, "You're sitting on the mop bucket."

This guy walks into the lounge, sits down and orders a scotch. He swigs it down, looks in his pocket, cringes, and then orders another. He gulps it down, looks in his pocket again and cringes again. Then he orders another one.

After a couple hours of this, the bartender says, "I know it's none of my business pal, but I got to ask. What do you keep looking at in your pocket?"

"Oh that," says the guy. "That's a picture of my wife. I drink until she starts to look good. Then I know it's time for me to go back to my cabin."

THE NEWLYWED
NOT-SO-NEWLYWED GAME

This guy comes home early one day and says to his wife, "Honey, pack your bags. I just won the lottery."

His wife says, "That's wonderful! Should I pack for warm weather or cold weather?"

"Whatever you like," he says. "Just as long as you're out of the house by noon."

A middle-aged guy and his wife are sunning themselves on deck. While the guy is reading the newspaper, his wife is busy commenting on a young couple across the pool.

"Look at them," she says. "They seem so devoted to each other. It's so cute the way he sneaks up behind her and kisses her on the neck. Why don't you ever do that?"

"Well, for one thing," he says, looking up from his paper, "I hardly know the woman."

A young couple went on a honeymoon cruise. The first night, while they were getting ready for bed, the groom handed his jeans to his bride and said, "Try these on."

"Honey," she said. "These are never going to fit me."

"That's right," he said, "and they never will. Remember, it's the man's job to wear the pants in the family."

"I see," she said, taking off her jeans. "Here, try these on."

He laughed and said, "I can't get into your pants."

"That's right," she said, "and until you change your attitude, you never will!"

This couple is sitting in the dining room when, all of a sudden, the guy slides under the table.

The waiter walks over and says, "Excuse me, ma'am, but your husband just slid under the table."

"He did not," says the lady. "My husband just came through that door."

This guy and his buddy go to the spa for a sauna. As they're getting undressed, he notices his friend is wearing a girdle.

He says, "So how long have you been wearing a girdle?"

"Ever since my wife found it in my glove compartment."

Muriel and her husband, Oscar, were sitting on deck one day when a young couple walked by with quintuplets.

"Isn't that something?" said Muriel. "Did you know that only happens once in four million times?"

"Really?" said Oscar, scratching his head. "When did they ever find the time to go to work?"

The Cruise Director sends a bottle of champagne to a couple's table in honor of their fiftieth wedding anniversary..

The husband stands up and proposes a toast to his wife, "This woman has always been there for me.. Through all the troubles and all the bad times, she was there. When I got fired from my job, she was there. When my business went down the toilet, she was there. When we lost our house in that fire, she was there. When I had that heart attack and almost died, she was there."

He pauses for a moment, then turns to his wife and says, "Come to think of it — maybe you're just bad luck."

> **"Women's faults are many.**
> **Men have only two.**
> **Everything thing they say**
> **And everything they do."**

This guy and his wife are having dinner with a newlywed couple they met onboard. The whole evening, the guy's wife monopolizes the conversation. She tells the young bride and groom everything they did that day and the sights they saw and all the stuff they bought, and so on -- and the whole time she's talking, her husband keeps yawning.

The new bride is so offended by the guy's behavior that, when his wife excuses herself to go to the bathroom, she confronts him, "I know we just met and I'm probably out of line. But I can't believe you could sit there, yawning, the whole time your wife was talking. That is so rude."

The guy looks at her and says, "I wasn't yawning. I was just trying to get a word in edgewise."

How do you keep your husband from reading your email?
Rename the folder, Instruction Manual.

Why does the female black widow kill the male after mating?
To stop the snoring before it begins."

A woman shows up for breakfast with a scowl on her face.
The waiter says, "Did you wake up grumpy this morning?"
She says, "No, I let him sleep."

A guy says, "I haven't spoken to my wife in years."
His friend asks, "Why not?"
He says, "I don't want to interrupt her."

"Men are like fine wine. They start out like grapes, and it's a woman's job to stomp on them and keep them in the dark until they mature into something you'd like to have dinner with."

Why are married women heavier than single women?
Single women come home, see what's in the fridge and go to bed. Married women come home, see what's in bed and go to the fridge.

On their twenty-fifth wedding anniversary, this guy asks his wife, "What would you like? A diamond necklace? A sable coat? A Caribbean cruise?"
She says, "I want a divorce."
He says, "I wasn't planning on spending that much."

A newlywed couple, David and Lisa were taking a cruise with David's parents. One afternoon, Lisa's mother-in-law went to the gift shop and bought her two scarves, one red and one blue.

That night, Lisa dressed for dinner in a beautiful blue gown, matching heels and, of course, the blue scarf her mother-in-law had purchased for her that afternoon.

When they arrived at the dinner table, her mother-in-law looked at her and said, "So you don't like the pink scarf?"

"I never knew what happiness was until I got married. Then it was too late."

The cruise was overbooked and a man and woman, who never met before, end up having to share a cabin with a double bed. When they get to their room, the woman says, "Since we're not married, I don't think it's right for us to sleep in the same bed. Would you mind sleeping on the floor?"

The guy says okay and makes his bed on the floor. Later that night, as he's just about to fall asleep, the woman says, "I hate to bother you, but it's awfully cold. Since you're closer to the closet, would you mind getting me another blanket."

So he gets her another blanket and settles back down to go to sleep. A little while later, she says, "I'm still terribly cold. I hate to trouble you, but I could really use another blanket?"

The guy gets her another blanket. A few minutes later, she says, "I'm still so terribly cold. Look, I know we're not married, but perhaps for just this one night we could pretend to be married. What do you think?"

"Fine with me," says the guy. "Get your own blanket!"

An elderly man is sitting by himself on the pool deck with a big smile on his face. The cruise director passes by and says, "You seem to be having a great time on this cruise."

The old man says, "I'm celebrating my divorce. For seventy years, my wife and I fought like cats and dogs, with never a moment's peace, and we finally decided to call it quits."

"If it was so bad, why didn't you get a divorce any sooner?"

"We wanted to wait until the kids were dead."

"Dear, if I died, would you get married again?"

"Definitely not!"

"You don't you like being married?"

" Of course I do."

"Then why wouldn't you get married again?"

" Okay, I'd get married again."

"Would you let her sleep in our bed?"

"Where else would she sleep?"

"Would you let her cook in my kitchen?"

" Where else would she cook?"

"And would you let her use my golf clubs?"

"Of course not. She's left-handed."

An old guy is sitting in the lobby, crying. The Cruise Director goes over and asks him, "What's the matter?"

He says, "I just got married to a twenty-five-year-old woman. She's beautiful, she's sexy, she's smart, and right now she's in my cabin waiting for me."

"So why are you crying?"

"I forgot my room number?"

This guy is sitting in his cabin, waiting for his wife to get dressed for the evening, when she says, "Darling, what do you think of my hair? Doesn't it look lovely this way?"

"Yes, dear."

"And my dress? Doesn't it do wonders for my figure?"

"Yes, dear."

"And don't these earrings bring out the blue in my eyes?

"Yes, dear."

"And don't these heels make my legs look long and shapely?

"Yes, dear."

"Oh, Sweetheart," she says, "you say the nicest things."

What do you call it when the husband gets in the last word at the end of an argument?

The beginning of a new argument.

Two guys are sitting on deck, having a beer.

The first one says, "My wife's an angel."

The second one says, "You're lucky. Mine's still alive."

**"This is my second marriage.
Same sentence, different warden."**

A lady goes to the purser's desk to report that her husband is missing. She says, "I'm looking for a man who is tall, well-built and handsome, with dark, wavy hair and a sweet disposition."

Her friend says, "What are you talking about? Your husband is short, fat, bald and the grumpiest man I ever met."

"Yes, I know," she says, "but why would I want him back?"

Dave and his wife, Julia, take a cruise for their twenty-fifth wedding anniversary. On the first night, they are seated with this obnoxious real estate developer and his young trophy wife.

When dinner is finally over, Dave turns to his wife and says, "I'll never understand how the biggest jerks always marry the most attractive women."

To which she replies, "Why, thank you, dear."

Retirement: Half the pay. Twice the husband.

Two ladies, Beatrice and Harriet, were talking by the pool. Harriet said, "I thought this cruise would put the romance back in our marriage, but it's not working. All my husband, Bob, ever thinks about is eating and drinking and gambling."

"That's too bad," said Beatrice. "After twenty-five years of marriage, my Sidney is still as romantic as the day we met."

"What is your secret?" asked Harriet.

"Well, I'll tell you," said Beatrice, "every day, when my Sidney comes home from the office, I greet him at the door wearing nothing but my birthday suit."

"Oh my!" said Harriet. "That sounds like a marvelous idea! And if it'll put the spark back into our love life, it's worth a try!"

Later that evening, when he returned from the casino, Bob was more than a little surprised to discover his wife standing in the middle of their cabin, buck naked.

"What on earth are you doing?" he asked.

"I'm wearing my birthday suit," she said in her most sultry voice. "What do you think?"

"Needs pressing," he said. "Let's eat."

The cabin steward showed a couple to their room. After helping the man with his luggage, he asks, "Is there anything else you need, sir?"

The guy says, "No, thank you."

"Maybe something for your wife?"

"Yeah. Thanks for the reminder. Do you guys sell post cards?"

In the gift shop, a customer spent half the day searching for an anniversary card.

Noticing the man lingering over one card after another, the clerk finally went over to see if she could help.

"Are you having a problem finding a card that expresses what you want to say?" she asked.

"No really," he said. "I'm just having a problem finding one that she'll believe."

"My wife just went to a self-help group for compulsive talkers. It's called On & On Anon."

The waiter noticed this older couple in the dining room who were particularly loving toward one another all week long. He was especially impressed by the way the husband always referred to his wife with such endearing terms as "Honey" and "Darling," and "Sweetheart."

One night, while the wife was powdering her nose, the waiter leaned over to him and said, "I think it's wonderful that, after all these years, you still use such loving terms for your wife."

"Well, to tell you the truth," said the old gent, "I forgot her name about 10 years ago!"

For their fiftieth wedding anniversary, Harold and Margaret, decided to go on a cruise. The first morning, they had room service deliver breakfast in bed.

"Oh Harold, this is so romantic. It's like being newlyweds again," said Margaret. "My bosom feels all warm and tingly."

"I'm not surprised," said Harold, "you've got one hanging in your coffee and the other one's in your oatmeal."

George, age 92, and Edith, age 89, meet on a cruise and decide to get married. On their way home from the airport, they pass by a drugstore. They go in and George asks the man behind the counter, "Are you the owner?"

The pharmacist answers, "Yes."

George says, "Do you sell heart medication?"

The Pharmacist says, "Of course we do."

"How about support hose for circulation?"

"Definitely."

"And medicine for rheumatism and arthritis?"

"All kinds."

"How about adult diapers?"

"Yes sir."

"Hearing aids and reading glasses?"

"Yes."

"What about eye drops, sleeping pills and Geritol?"

"Absolutely."

"You sell wheelchairs, walkers and canes?"

"All kinds and sizes. Why all of these questions?"

George smiles and says, "We're getting married soon and we'd like to use your store as our Bridal Registry."

Two guys are sitting by the pool. One says to the other, "My wife is very touchy. We argue constantly. The least little thing I do just sets her off."

The other one says, "You're lucky. Mine's a self-starter."

A guy was hanging around in the gift shop, trying to decide what to get his wife for their anniversary, when his friend said, "She already has everything you could think of. She doesn't need more stuff. Why don't you just make up a gift certificate that says: Thirty minutes of great loving, any way you like it."

So the guy thanked his friend and went back to his cabin.

The next day, when they met for lunch, the guy's friend asked, "Did your wife like your present?"

The guy said, "She sure did. She jumped up, kissed me on the cheek, and then she ran out the door yelling, 'See you in half an hour!'"

How to impress a woman? Wine her, dine her, caress her, hold her, comfort her, listen to her, care for her and share with her, stand by her and support her, and never let her go.

How to impress a man? Show up naked. Bring beer.

Two guys were about to tee off when a funeral procession went by. The first guy stopped, took off his hat and bowed his head until the last car went by. Then he lined up his shot.

The second guy said, "Wow, I didn't realize what a sensitive person you were, noticing that funeral and everything."

"It's the least I could do," said the first guy, "We would have been married 25 years tomorrow."

A guy and his wife were killed in an automobile accident. When they get to heaven, they are escorted to a big mansion with a swimming pool and beautiful gardens and dozens of servants who cater to their every whim. Everything is perfect and yet the husband is scowling.

His wife says, "What's wrong?"

He says, "You know, if it wasn't for your stupid oat bran, we could have been here years ago."

A couple were celebrating their twenty-fifth anniversary. When the people at their table suggested a toast, the wife looked at her husband. Then she punched him in the shoulder and said, "That's for 25 years of bad sex."

The husband thought for a moment. Then he punched her in the shoulder and said, "That's for knowing the difference."

THE
LOVE BOAT

This guy decides to take his wife on a cruise for their fiftieth wedding anniversary. He goes to the drugstore and asks the pharmacist for some Viagra and some seasick pills.

The pharmacist shakes his head and says, "Gee, if it makes you that sick, why do it?"

Late one night, the security officer hears a racket coming from inside one of the lifeboats. He opens the hatch and shines his flashlight on a couple who are making love. He says, "What do you people think you're doing?"

The guy says, "I'm making love to my wife."

The security officer says, "This is a public place. Can't you do that in your cabin?"

The guy says, "If you must know, I didn't realize it was my wife until you shined that flashlight on her."

This guy shuffles up the ship's priest and says, "Father, I'm eighty years old. I got five kids and eleven grandchildren. Last night, I had an affair with a woman half my age."

The priest says, "Are you Catholic?"

He says, "No, Father, I'm not."

"Then why are you telling me?"

"Oh, I'm telling everybody!"

A middle-aged bachelor approaches a 20-year-old girl in the disco and says, "Where have you been all my life?"

She says, "Well, for the first half of it, I wasn't born yet."

> **"Give me a beach,**
> **a sunset and a beautiful woman**
> **and you can keep the beach**
> **and the sunset."**

An old woman is walking along the beach with her dog when she sees a magic lamp buried in the sand. When she rubs the lamp, a genie appears and says, "I'm granting you three wishes."

The woman says, "I wish I were young and beautiful again."

Poof! She's young and beautiful.

She says, "I wish I was wealthy beyond my wildest dreams."

Poof! A trunk full of money appears.

For her final wish, she says, "I wish my faithful dog, Spot, was a handsome, young man who was deeply in love with me."

Poof! The dog is transformed into a handsome young man.

He takes her in his arms, kisses her passionately and says, "Now, darling, aren't you sorry you took me to the vet?"

One day, it's very crowded by the pool. A young woman in a bikini walks over to this guy and says, "Excuse me, sir, but would you mind giving up your chair for a pregnant lady?"

The guy looks her over and says, "You don't look pregnant."

She says, "Well, it's only been about half an hour."

**"Lead me not into temptation.
I can find the way myself."**

Bill comes back to his cabin one afternoon to find his wife sitting naked on the edge of the bed.

He says, "Honey, why aren't you dressed?"

She says, "I don't have anything to wear."

"Don't be silly," he says. "You've got lots of clothes."

Then he goes over to the closet, opens the door and says, "Honey, look — here's a pink dress, here's a green dress, here's the cabin steward, here's that black dress …"

A couple is on a cruise with their ten-year-old son, Michael. After several days, they're feeling quite amorous, but they can't seem to find any "alone time."

So they send Michael out on the balcony and tell him to give them a running commentary on all the sights he can see.

Michael says, "There's some dolphins swimming by the ship, and the cruise ship next to us is getting ready to pull up anchor, and the people in the cabin below us are having sex."

His parents bolt upright in bed and say, "How can you tell the people below us are having sex?"

"Because their kid is standing outside on the balcony, too."

This guy is sitting in the lounge one night. This lady walks up and says, "I want you to make me feel like a real woman."

He takes off his jacket and says, "Here. This needs ironing."

This guy goes up to the pool deck to get some sun. When he gets there, he sees a gorgeous redhead, reading a magazine. He takes the chair next to her and asks her what she's reading.

She says, "Oh, it's a fascinating article all about the mating rituals of different ethnic groups around the world."

"Really?" he says, "Like what?"

"Oh, lots of stuff," she says. "Like, for instance, did you know that Native American men make the most sensitive mates, and Polish men are considered to be the most passionate?"

"No, I didn't," he says. "That is fascinating."

"By the way, my name is Sarah," she says. "What's yours?"

"Tonto Kowalski."

DIARY OF A YOUNG WOMAN ON A CRUISE SHIP

Dear Diary,

MONDAY: What a wonderful cruise this is going to be! The staff is so friendly. The Captain even asked me to dine at his table tonight.

TUESDAY: The Captain asked me to spend the afternoon with him on the bridge.

WEDNESDAY: The Captain made a proposal to me that was unbecoming an officer and a gentleman.

THURSDAY: The Captain threatened to sink the ship if I do not give in to his indecent proposals!

FRIDAY: This afternoon I saved 1600 lives.

While getting onto a crowded elevator, one of the cruise staff accidentally elbowed an elderly lady in the bosom.

"I'm terribly sorry, ma'am," said the flustered young man, "but if the rest of you is as soft as your bosom, I'm sure you'll find it in your heart to forgive me."

"Certainly," she replied. "And if the rest of you is as hard as your elbow, I'm in Cabin 414."

This lady was sitting in the lounge, sharing a drink with a strange man. After awhile, she said, "I better warn you, my husband will be back from his snorkeling trip in about an hour."

"But I haven't done anything I shouldn't do."

"I know. So, if you're going to, you better hurry up."

"A Caribbean cruise is a lot like sex. When it's good, it's really good. And when it's bad, it's still pretty good."

A lady passenger was walking on deck when her glass eye fell out and rolled down the stairs. A man grabbed it and brought it back to her. She thanked him and asked if he'd like to have dinner with her.

He said, "That's very nice, but do you ask every man you meet to dinner?"

"No," she said, "only the ones who catch my eye."

A guy goes up to the ship's chaplain and says, "Do you think it's okay to have sex before you're married."

The chaplain says, "Not if it delays the ceremony."

Bill, Fred and Jim were discussing their love lives when Bill said, "My wife and I average two, maybe three times a week."

Fred said, "For my wife and I, it's maybe twice a week."

Jim smiled and said, "For my wife and I, it's only once a year."

"Once a year?" said Bill. "Then why the big smile?"

"Because tonight's the night!"

This older couple is at the Captain's Cocktail Party when the husband starts flirting with some younger women.

The captain says to the wife, "Doesn't it bother you that your husband is over there making passes at the younger women?"

"Not really," says the wife. "Dogs chase cars, but that doesn't mean they know how to drive."

"A clear conscience is the sign of a bad memory."

A couple took a cruise for their fiftieth wedding anniversary. One afternoon while her husband was napping, the wife slipped on her black silk negligee. Then she tiptoed over to her husband and whispered in his ear, "Super sex! Super sex!"

Her husband opened his eyes and said, "I'll have the soup."

This ninety-year-old guy took his eighteen-year-old bride on a cruise for their honeymoon. On their first night together, he said to her, "Honey, do you remember everything your mother told you was going to happen on this night?"

She said, "Yes I do."

He said, "Good, because I've completely forgotten."

A ninety-year-old bachelor sees his eighty-year-old girlfriend at breakfast. He says, "My memory is slipping. Did I ask you to marry me last night?"

"Well, someone did," she said. "I just can't remember who."

A ninety-year-old gentleman takes his young bride on a cruise for their honeymoon. He books adjoining rooms because he's afraid his loud snoring will keep her awake.

After dinner, the fellow gets out his prescription of Viagra. Since it will be their first night together, he takes an extra dose to be certain he won't disappoint his young wife.

While his young bride's getting ready for bed, there's a knock on her door. She opens it and sees her husband standing there with a sheepish grin on his face. So she invites him in, they have a wonderful time and, afterwards, he returns to his room.

About an hour later, she hears another knock. She opens the door and to her surprise, he's back. So she invites him in again. They have a wonderful time and he returns to his room.

An hour later, another knock and once more, he's standing at the door with a sheepish grin. Shocked at his amazing stamina, she says, "Oh dear, I can't believe you came back again."

He says, "I was here before?"

A couple celebrated their fiftieth wedding anniversary by taking an around-the-world cruise.

On the first night, the wife said, "Do you remember when we were first married, how you used to take my hand and kiss me on the cheek and nibble on my ear lobe?"

"I sure do," said her husband, "Let me go get my teeth."

How can you tell the newlyweds on a cruise?

They're the ones without the tan.

Larry and Barbara go on a Halloween cruise. Barbara packs costumes for both of them and is very excited about dressing up for the celebration.

However, when Halloween night arrives, Barbara is feeling a bit under the weather and Larry has to go alone.

Larry gets into his gorilla suit and leaves for the party. After a short nap, Barbara is feeling much better. Realizing that Larry hasn't seen her costume, she decides it might be fun to show up at the party and see how her husband acts when she's not around.

When she arrives, she sees Larry in his gorilla suit, dancing, drinking and flirting with several different ladies.

When Barbara comes over, he starts to flirt with her. They dance several dances and then he suggests they go outside for a little walk on the promenade deck. Barbara agrees, and soon they find themselves making love by the pool.

Later, Barbara hurries back to their cabin and waits to see what Larry has to say about his evening.

A few hours later, he returns and finds Barbara sitting up and reading in bed.

She asks, "So, how was your evening, dear?"

"Oh, nothing special," he says with a shrug. "You know I never have a good time when you're not around."

"Didn't you even dance?"

"No," he says. "In fact, I spent the entire evening playing cards in the casino. But the fellow I loaned my costume to said he had a heck of a good time."

Two widows, Sophie and Ruth, were in the lounge one night when they spied a distinguished gentleman sitting alone at the bar. Ruth went over to strike up a conversation.

"You look kind of lonely sitting here all by yourself," she said.

"I guess I should look lonely," he replied. "I spent the last twenty years in prison."

"Really? Why were you in prison?" asked Ruth.

"For murdering my wife," he said.

"Really," said Ruth. "Well, it was nice chatting with you."

"Same here," said the man.

When Ruth returned, Sophie said, "What did you find out?"

"Well for one thing," said Ruth, "he's single."

This guy is returning to his cabin one evening when his neighbor stops him and says, "Boy, you are one noisy neighbor. I heard you and your wife making whoopie all afternoon."

The guy says, "Oh yeah? Well, the joke's on you. I wasn't even here this afternoon!"

On their honeymoon night, the groom says, "Honey, am I the first man you ever made love with?"

"Why does everyone keep asking me that?"

"I met this wonderful man on my last cruise," Barbara told her friend. "He was cute and sensitive and a great listener. It seemed like a perfect relationship, but then he said something that broke my heart."

"What was that?" asked her friend.

"No hablo ingles."

Before going on a cruise with her parents, a college coed bought a skimpy bikini and modeled it for her mother.

"What do you think?" she asked.

"Well," said her mother, "if I'd worn that bathing suit when I was your age, you'd be four years older than you are now."

A seventy-year-old millionaire boarded the ship with his twenty-year-old trophy wife.

"You crafty, old codger," said one of his ship mates, "how did you ever convince her to marry you?"

"Easy," he said, "I told her I was 95."

THE
S.S. GERITOL

One evening, this older fellow's telling the Cruise Director about his day in port. He says, "My wife and I went to this wonderful little restaurant for lunch and I can't remember the name of it. It's uh ... what's the name of that flower with the sharp thorns that can be either red, white or pink?"

The Cruise Director says, "Rose."

"Yeah," he says, turning to his wife, "Rose, what's the name of that restaurant we went to today?"

This fellow went to the doctor and said, "I'm going on a cruise. There's probably going to be a lot of young, available women. The problem is, my sex drive is too high. I want it lowered."

The doctor said, "You're eighty years old and you think your sex drive is too high? Trust me, it's all in your head."

"I know," said the old man. "I want it lowered."

Three senior citizens were discussing their health problems.

The first one said, "I get up every morning at seven and it takes me half an hour to pee."

The second one said, " I get up every morning at eight and it takes me half an hour to have a bowel movement."

"Oh I don't have that problem," said the third one. "Every morning, it's like clockwork. At seven, I pee like a racehorse. At eight, I have a bowel movement like you wouldn't believe."

"So what's your problem?"

"I don't wake up till nine!"

"God grant me the senility to forget the people I never liked, the good fortune to run into the ones I do, and the eyesight to tell the difference."

A couple is in the dining room, celebrating their fiftieth wedding anniversary.

When they finish dessert, the wife winks at her husband and says, "Let's run upstairs and make love."

Her husband says, "Pick one. I can't do both."

Have you seen the new slot machines for older passengers?

Three prunes means you've hit the jackpot.

An old lady goes to the Singles Get Together and announces to the group, "Whoever can guess what I have in my hand gets to spend the night with me."

A fellow in the back yells out, "An elephant!"

She says, "Close enough! Let's go!"

A couple, in their nineties, are sitting by the pool. They order drinks and when the waiter arrives with them, the wife turns to her husband and says, "I forgot my sunscreen. Would you be a dear and get it for me."

He says, "Okay, but don't start drinking without me."

"I wouldn't dream of it," she says. "Now get my sunscreen."

An hour later, the woman's throat is parched. When she reaches for her glass, her husband says, "Look, if you're going to start drinking without me, then I'm not going."

Two older passengers are sitting by the pool. One says to the other, "I'm 83 years old now and I'm full of aches and pains. You look about my age. How do you feel?"

"Like a newborn baby."

"Really? Like a baby!"

"Yep. No hair, no teeth, and I think I just wet myself."

"I have a photographic memory. I'm just out of film."

This old gent is worried that his wife was going deaf. So one day, at the buffet, he sneaks up behind her and says, "Do you want me to get you some coffee, dear?"

No answer.

He comes a little closer and says it again.

No answer.

Finally, he gets right up behind her and says, "Do you want me to get you some coffee, dear?"

She turns to him and says, "For the third time, yes!"

A couple took their eleven-year-old grandson, Jeffrey, on a cruise with them. Since it was during the school year, Jeffrey's parents reminded them that he would still have to spend at least one hour a day doing his homework.

One afternoon, while Jeffrey was working on a math assignment, he said, "Grandpa, do you think you could help me with the answer to this one?"

"I could," said Grandpa, "but it wouldn't be right, would it?"

"Well, probably not," said Jeffrey, "but why don't you take a shot at it, anyway?"

Old is when you have the choice of two temptatations and you choose the one that will get you to bed earlier.

When grandma returned from her cruise, she brought a present for each of her two grandsons. When they opened their gifts and discovered water pistols, the boys squealed with delight and headed for the nearest sink.

Their mother was not so pleased, however. She turned to grandma and said, "I'm surprised at you, mother. Don't you remember when we were kids, how we used to drive you crazy playing with water guns?"

Grandma smiled and said, "Of course I remember ..."

A ninety-year-old passenger booked a honeymoon cruise and said to the travel agent, "I'm marrying an eighteen-year-old college co-ed."

"Aren't you worried that could be fatal?" asked the agent.

"Well," shrugged the old guy, "If she dies, she dies."

A lady goes to the purser's desk to report that her husband is missing. When the purser asks her to describe him, the lady says, ""Well, he's short and bald. He's got an artificial hip, a hearing aid, and he wears dentures. Come to think of it, most of him was missing before he was."

YOU'RE GETTING OLDER WHEN...

YOUR KNEES BUCKLE BUT YOUR BELT WON'T.

THAT GLEAM IN YOUR EYE IS FROM
THE SUN HITTING YOUR BIFOCALS.

YOU SINK YOUR TEETH INTO A STEAK
AND THEY STAY THERE.

YOU NAP BY THE POOL AND PEOPLE
STOP TO CHECK YOUR VITAL SIGNS

YOU CAN LIVE WITHOUT SEX
BUT NOT WITHOUT YOUR GLASSES

YOU ACTUALLY ENJOY HEARING
ABOUT OTHER PEOPLE'S OPERATIONS

YOU PARTY IN YOUR CABIN AND
YOUR NEIGHBORS DON'T NOTICE

YOU DON'T HAVE TO BE DOING
SOMETHING TO GET INJURED

WHAT DOESN'T HURT, DOESN'T WORK

Two ladies on a Single Seniors Cruise:
"How was your date last night?"
"Oh, I had to slap the fellow's face!"
"Why? Did he try to go too far?"
"No. I thought he was dead."

Two retired professors are sunbathing by the pool. One says to the other, "By the way, old friend, have you read Marx?"
"Yes," says the other, "I believe it's from these wicker chairs."

Postcard from Grandpa: Having a good time. Where am I?

A gentleman took his grandchildren on a cruise. The first night, as they were getting ready for bed, he took his teeth out and put them in a glass of water on the nightstand.

"Grandpa," said his little grandson. "You shouldn't put your teeth there."

"Why not?" asked Grandpa.

"Well, if you put them under your pillow, we can pay for the whole cruise."

After a guest lecture on wills and estates, three older fellows are discussing how they'd like to be remembered. The first one says, "When I am laid out in my casket, I'd like my friends and loved ones to say I was a good husband and father."

The second guy says, "I'd like them to say I was a great doctor and humanitarian."

The third guy says, "I'd like them to say, Look, he's moving!"

A retired guy was walking along the beach when he came across a small green frog. When he stopped and picked it up, the frog began to speak.

"I'm a talking frog," said the frog.

"That's amazing," said the old man.

"Even more amazing," said the frog, "not only can I talk but I'm magical as well. If you kiss me, I will turn into a beautiful blonde woman."

"Hmm," said the old man. Then he put the frog in his pocket and began to walk along.

After a minute, the frog stuck his head out of the fellow's pocket and said, "Didn't you hear me? If you kiss me, I will turn into a beautiful, blonde woman."

"I heard you," said the old man. "It's just that, at my age, sometimes you prefer a talking frog."

"Age doesn't always bring wisdom. Sometimes it shows up empty handed."

Two older passengers are sitting next to each other at the bar. The first one says, "Hi, my name's Bob. What's yours?"

The second one thinks for a moment, then mouths something to himself as he gently rocks back and forth.

Finally, he stops and says, "My name is Lester. Pleased to meet you."

"Likewise, I'm sure," says Bob. "I don't mean to be nosy, but what were you doing just then?"

"Oh that," says Lester. "I was just remembering that song, 'Happy birthday to you, happy birthday to you …'"

This guy is walking through the buffet when he is stopped by a fellow who says, "Jeff! Jeff Johnson! I can't believe it's you! Last time I saw you, you were thirty pounds lighter and had a full head of hair! Now you're fat and bald and you wear glasses!"

The guy says, "I don't know what you're talking about, pal. My name is Leonard Miller."

"Really -- you changed your name, too?"

A BIRTHDAY TOAST
Another candle on your cake,
There's no need to pout.
Be glad that you still got the strength
To blow the darn thing out!

Mabel was widowed after sixty-five years of marriage. Her children sent her on a cruise to take her mind off things.

She went on the cruise, but the plan didn't work. She was more lonesome than ever. Finally she decided to end it all and join her beloved in death.

Thinking it would be best to get it over with quickly, she bought a pistol and ammunition to shoot herself in her broken heart. Not wanting to miss this vital organ and end up a vegetable and a burden to her children, she went to the ship's doctor and asked him exactly where the heart was located.

"On a woman," said the unsuspecting doctor, "the heart is on the left side just below the breast."

Mabel thanked him and went back to her cabin.

Later that night, Mabel was taken to the infirmary where she was treated for a bullet wound in her left knee.

PARTY GAMES FOR SENIOR CRUISERS

SAG! YOU'RE IT!

PIN THE TOUPEE ON THE BALD GUY

20 QUESTIONS SHOUTED IN YOUR GOOD EAR

KICK THE BUCKET

RED ROVER, RED ROVER, THE NURSE SAYS BEND OVER

DOC, DOC, GOOSE

SIMON SAYS SOMETHING INCOHERENT

MUSICAL RECLINERS

SPIN THE BOTTLE OF GERITOL

HIDE AND GO NAP!

Bill was celebrating his retirement by taking his wife, Julie, on a cruise. One night while they were walking along the deck, a seagull flew over and pooped on the his head.

"Oh dear!" said Julie. "Let me get some toilet paper."

"Never mind," said Bill, "he's probably miles away by now."

Two matrons were sitting by the pool. After several hours, one turns to the other and says, "You know, I've been sitting here so long, my butt fell asleep!."

The other one says, "I know! I heard it snoring!"

An old lady was standing at the ship's railing, both hands holding onto her hat to keep it from blowing off.

Unfortunately the wind was blowing her skirt up, revealing everything underneath.

A deckhand, who was passing by, said, "Excuse me, ma'am. I don't mean to embarrass you, but standing that way, you are completely exposed?"

"Oh honey," she said, "what you are looking at is eighty seven years old — the hat is brand new."

SENIOR MOTTO
Seen it all, done it all,
Can't remember most of it.

A widower, in his eighties, was getting ready to go on his first cruise. His friends suggested he purchase some Viagra. He went to the pharmacy and asked, "Does it really work?"

"Oh yes, one of these will make you feel like a man of thirty."

"Can I get it over the counter?"

"Well, for that, you'll probably need two."

Grandpa's health was failing so his family decided to send him on a two week Caribbean cruise.

Near the end of the cruise, Grandpa passed away and the cruise line shipped him back home.

At the funeral, his family gathered to pay their last respects. One of the relatives said, "Doesn't he look wonderful?"

"Yes," replied another relative. "That two weeks in the Caribbean did him a world of good."

One day, a family brought their elderly grandmother up to sit by the pool while they went off snorkeling.

Before they left, they asked the cruise staff to keep an eye on her while they were gone.

That afternoon, the staff went out of their way to make sure she had everything she needed. They brought her drinks, served her lunch, and set her in a chair overlooking the beach.

Everything went smoothly until someone noticed she was starting to lean sideways in her chair. A deckhand rushed over to catch her and straighten her back up. For a few minutes everything was fine, but then she started to tilt to the other side. Again the deckhand rushed over and set her upright. A little bit later, she tilted again, and again the deckhand set her right. This went on all afternoon.

Later, when her family returned from their snorkeling trip, her grandson asked her, "So grandma, how was your day? Did they treat you all right?"

"Oh, everyone was very nice," she said, "except they won't let you fart."

Two old timers decide play a round of golf. When they get to the first tee, one says to the other, "My eyesight isn't what it used to be. Can you keep an eye on my ball for me?"

The other one says, "Sure! I see fine. Go ahead and hit."

So the first guy steps up to the tee and hits the ball. Then he turns to the other guy and says, "Did you see where it went?"

He says, "Sure did!"

"Well, where did it go?"

"I can't remember."

One of the older passengers says to another, "My teeth are gone, my digestion's terrible, my joints ache, but at least my mind is still here, knock wood."

Then he looks around and says, "Who's there?"

A retired couple is sitting by the pool when the husband turns to his wife and says, "You want to go for a walk?"

She says, "No, it's too windy."

He says, "No, it's Thursday."

She says, "Me too. Let's order a drink."

This older fellow is going to get ice cream, so he offers to get something for his wife as well.

She says, "Okay, I'll have a bowl of ice cream. Vanilla. Do you want to write this down so you can remember it?"

He says, "No, I can remember it."

She says, "Okay then, I also want some strawberries on top. Maybe you should write this down so you don't forget.

He says, "No, I'll remember."

She says, "I would also like some whipped cream on top. Are you sure you don't want to write this down? I know you're going to forget."

He says, "I don't need to write it down. I can remember just fine. You want a bowl of vanilla ice cream with strawberries and whipped cream."

Then he goes off to the buffet. Twenty minutes later, he comes back with a plate of bacon and eggs.

His wife says, "Just like I thought. You forgot the toast."

LAUGHTER IS THE BEST MEDICINE

The first day of the cruise, a guy is sitting in the doctor's office, looking quite ill. The nurse looks at him and says, "Flu?"

The guy looks up and says, "Yes, all the way from Dallas!"

A woman took her sick husband to see the ship's doctor. After examining him, the doctor came out to the waiting room and said, "Frankly, ma'am, I don't like the looks of your husband."

"Neither do I," replied the woman, "but he's awfully good with the children."

This old timer goes in to see the ship's doctor. He says, "I think I'm going deaf."

The doctor examines him and says, "You're not going deaf. You've got a suppository stuck in your ear."

"Well, now I know what happened to my hearing aid."

A ninety-year-old man went to the ship's doctor complaining of chest pains.

The doctor asked, "Do you still have a sex life?"

"Yes, I do," said the old man.

"Then I would recommend you give up half your sex life," said the doctor.

"Which half?" he asked. "The looking or the thinking?"

A guy goes to the ship's doctor, complaining of headaches. After examining him, the doctor says, "What you have is called a tension headache. I used to have the same problem. I found the best cure for it was to go to my cabin and make love to my wife. Why don't you try that and let me know how it goes?"

The guy says thanks and goes on his way.

A few hours later the doctor sees the guy out on deck, looking much better. So he stops and asks him how he's doing.

The guy says, "Never better. My headache's gone. I never felt more relaxed. That was certainly the perfect cure — and by the way, doctor, you have a lovely cabin."

An old fellow suddenly took ill and his son took him to the ship's infirmary. After the doctor treated the fellow, he allowed the son to visit him.

As the son stood at his bedside, the father began to breathe heavily and grabbed the pen and pad by the bed. With his last ounce of strength, he scribbled a note and handed it to his son.

At the funeral, the son decided to share his father's last words. He reached into his coat pocket, pulled out the note and read: YOU IDIOT — GET OFF MY OXYGEN HOSE!

A guy goes to the medical center and says, "Doc, I've got a problem. I read in a magazine how Vigoro could help your sex life, so I been taking some every day since I been on this cruise. The problem is, it hasn't done me a bit of good."

"Well for one thing," says the doctor, "you're supposed to be taking Viagra, not Vigoro. Vigoro is a fertilizer."

"Oh," says the guy. "Well, that explains the berries."

A guy goes to see the ship's doctor. He says, "Doc, I lost my memory."

"Really?" says the doctor, "When did this happen?"

"When did what happen?"

Another guy goes to see the doctor. The doctor says, "I'm sorry to tell you this, but you don't have much time left."

The guy says, "How long, doc?"

The doctor says, "Ten."

"Ten what? Days? Months? Years?"

"Ten … nine … eight … seven …"

A couple brought their little boy to the Medical Center. He was crying hysterically, but managed to tell the doctor that he swallowed a penny and was sure he was going to die.

The doctor tried to calm him but no amount of talking was helping. So the doctor palmed a penny from his pocket and pretended to pull it from the little boy's ear.

The boy was delighted. In a flash, he snatched it from the doctor's hand, swallowed it, and then cheerfully demanded, "Do it again, Doc!"

The ship's doctor says, "I have bad news, Mr. Johnson. You have cancer and you have Alzheimer's."

"Oh," says Mr. Johnson, "Well, at least I don't have cancer."

A guy goes to the medical center, complaining of stomach pains. The doctor examines him and says, "I can't figure out exactly what's wrong with you. I think it might be the result of too much heavy drinking."

"Well then," says the guy, "perhaps I should come back when you're sober."

An older passenger wasn't feeling well, so his wife took him to see the ship's doctor. Since the guy was hard-of-hearing, his wife acted as interpreter.

The doctor said, "I'd like to check your heart. Could you take off your shirt?"

The old man stared for a moment, then he turned to his wife and asked, "What did he say?"

His wife said loudly, "THEY WANT YOUR SHIRT!"

So he took off his shirt.

The doctor said, "Now, could you take off your socks? I would like to examine your feet."

"What did he say?" asked the old man.

His wife said, "THEY WANT YOUR SOCKS!"

So he took off his socks.

Then the doctor said, "Since you're here, I guess we should get a stool sample and a urine sample as well."

"What did he say?" asked the old man.

His wife said, "THEY WANT YOUR UNDERPANTS!"

A guy sees the ship's doctor. He says, "I don't know what's wrong. I hurt all over. If I touch my shoulder, it hurts. If I touch my leg, it hurts. If I touch my arm, it hurts."

"Simple," says the doctor, "You've broken your finger."

A lady goes to the doctor complaining of chest pains. The doctor says, "You have acute angina."

The lady says, "Why thank you, doctor."

One night, an old man goes to the doctor complaining about the rough seas. The doctor says, "We're all out of seasick pills, but I could let you have some Viagra."

"Will that cure seasickness?" asks the old man.

"No," says the doctor, "but it might keep you from rolling out of bed."

A guy goes to the ship's doctor. He says, "Doc, I can't pee."

The doctor says, "How old are you?"

The guys says, "Ninety-three."

The doctor says, "You've peed enough."

A lady goes to see the ship's doctor. She says, "Give it to me straight, Doc. What's wrong with my husband?"

The doctor says, "Your husband is in terrible shape. If you want him to live, you're going to have to change your lifestyle. From now on, you have to feed him right and make sure he gets plenty of sleep and wait on him hand and foot."

In the waiting room, her husband asks, "So what did he say?"

"He said you're going to die."

A old man went in to see the ship's doctor and said, "Doc, this rich food onboard has given me terrible gas. I can't control myself. Heck, since I walked in your office, I already broke wind twice. Fortunately they're not noisy or smelly, but it's still terribly embarrassing, nonetheless. Is there anything you can give me for it?"

The doctor wrote out a prescription and handed it to him. The old man looked at it and said, "Nose drops? What the heck are nose drops going to do?"

"Well," said the doctor, "first we're going work on your sense of smell, then we'll see about your hearing."

A guy shows up at the medical center with a cucumber in his left ear, a carrot in his right ear and a banana up his nose. He says, "Doc, what's wrong with me?"

"Simple," says the doctor, "you're not eating right."

A guy goes to the ship's doctor. The doctor says, "You're in perfect health. You'll live to be eighty."

The guy says, "But doc, I am eighty."

The doctor says, "See? What did I tell you?"

The Captain goes to see the ship's doctor.

"What's the matter?" asks the doctor.

The Captain says, "I've got a sore throat, stomach ache, and I think I'm running a temperature."

"Sounds like some kind of virus."

"Could be. Almost everyone in the crew has it."

"In that case, maybe it's some kind of staff infection."

A guy goes to see the ship's doctor because he's feeling tired and rundown. The doctor tells him that he has to give up sex.

The guy says, "But I'm a young guy. I'm in the prime of my life. How can I just give up sex?"

"Well," says the doctor, "just do what everybody does. Get married and taper off gradually."

A lady goes to the ship's doctor to see if anything can be done about her constipation.

"It's terrible," she says, "I haven't moved my bowels in a week."

"What have you done about it?" asks the doctor.

"Well," she says, "I sit in the bathroom for a half hour in the morning and a half hour again at night."

"No," says the doctor, "I mean do you take anything?"

"Naturally," she says, "I take a book."

A lady goes to see the ship's doctor. She says, "Doc, you got to help me. Every time I go to the bathroom nickels come out."

The doctor tells her to relax with her feet up, drink plenty of fluids and come back tomorrow.

The next day, she's back. "Doc, it's getting worse. Now every time I go to the bathroom, dimes come out."

Again, the doctor tells her to relax with her feet up, drink plenty of fluids and come back tomorrow.

The next day, the woman is beside herself, "Doc, I'm still not any better. In fact, now when I go to the bathroom, quarters come out! What the heck is wrong with me?"

The doctor says, "Relax, relax, you're just going through your change."

An old guy went to ship's doctor and said, "I need some Viagra and some Ginko."

"I know what you need the Viagra for," said the doctor, "but why the Ginko?"

"So I can remember why I took the Viagra."

"Honey, I just got back from the doctor. It was terrible."

"Why was that?"

"He said I was going to have to take this medicine every day for the rest of my life."

"Well, that's not so terrible."

"Oh yeah? He only gave me four pills."

A guy goes to see the ship's doctor and says, "Doc, my wife is a terrible woman. I've lived with her for almost thirty years. She nags me all the time. She's always criticizing me. And now, I think she's trying to poison me."

The doctor says, "Are you sure?"

The man says, "Yes, I'm almost certain she's trying to poison me. What should I do?"

"Tell you what," says the Doctor, "let me talk to her. I'll see what I can find out and let you know."

A few days later the Doctor calls the man and says, "Well, I spoke to your wife. In fact, I spoke to her on the phone for almost three hours. You want my advice?"

"Yes."

"Take the poison."

THAT'S ENTERTAINMENT

A magician worked on a cruise ship. Since the audience was always different, he did the same tricks over and over again.

The Captain had a pet parrot onboard who watched every show. Eventually the bird began to figure out the tricks. Once he understood how they were done, he began shouting out in the middle of the show, "It's not the same hat!" or "He's hiding the flowers under the table." or "The card's up his sleeve!"

The magician was furious. Late one night, he kidnapped the parrot, put him in a lifeboat, and left him there.

Three days later, the ship sank. The magician found himself in a lifeboat in the middle of the ocean, as fate would have it, with the parrot. They stared at each other with hatred but did not utter a word.

This went on day after day until finally the parrot said, "Okay, I give up, where's the ship?"

A hypnotist was doing a show on a cruise ship. He got several volunteers from the audience and brought them onstage. Then he started swinging his watch back and forth and said, "You're getting sleepy. Sleepy."

When the volunteers fell asleep, he said, "Now bark!"

They all barked in unison.

He said, "Meow!"

They all meowed like cats.

Just then, the ship hit a big wave. The hypnotist dropped his watch and said, "Aw, crap!"

Walking through the auditorium just before show time, the Captain noticed a man sprawled across three seats, mumbling incoherently. Assuming the man was drunk, he demanded, "Sir, where have come from?"

The man groaned, "The balcony."

Three guys are standing in line at the Pearly Gates. Saint Peter asks the first guy, "What was your salary?"

The guy says, "$200,000 a year."

Saint Peter says, "And what did you do for a living?"

The guy says, "I was a ship's captain."

Saint Peter asks the second guy, "What was your salary?"

The guy says, "$100,000 a year."

Saint Peter says, "And what did you do for a living?"

The guy says, "I was a Cruise Director."

Saint Peter asks the third guy, "What was your salary?"

The guy says, "$8,000 a year."

Saint Peter says, "Cool! What instrument did you play?"

A magician, performing on a cruise ship for the first time, was having a tough time getting the audience to respond.

He tried trick after trick, but nothing work. They just stared at him. Determined to impress them, the magician announced, "For my final trick, I will attempt something no magician has ever done before."

He picked a volunteer from the audience, a huge man with massive arms. He handed the guy a baseball bat and said, "I want you to hit me in the back of the head with this bat as hard as you can."

The guy was stunned, "I can't do that — you'll be killed!"

"Trust me," said the magician. "I'm a professional. I know what I'm doing."

"Well, okay," said the volunteer, shaking his head. Then he swung the bat as hard as he could and smacked the magician in the back of the head.

The magician went flying off the stage and landed in a heap on the front row, unconscious.

The audience was stunned. The ship's doctor was called but he could not revive him.

The next day, the magician was taken by helicopter to a nearby hospital where he remained in a coma for months. The doctors tried everything, but there was no sign of life. Finally, they decided to take him off life support.

His family came in to say goodbye. The priest gave him last rites. Then, just as they were about to pull the plug, a toe twitched. A finger moved slightly. An eyelid fluttered. Then, very slowly, the magician opened one eye, looked around the room, and whispered, "Tah dah."

A Midwestern couple were sitting in the atrium, enjoying a cocktail while a string quartet played in the background.

"It's a lovely concerto, isn't it?" said the wife.

"What?" said the husband.

"I said, 'It's a lovely concerto,'" she repeated.

"What?" said the husband.

"I said ... " she began again.

"Never mind," he said, "I can't hear you over all that racket."

On his way to the ship, a juggler was stopped by the local police. The cop looked at him and asked, "What are these matches and lighter fluid doing in your car?"

The juggler said, "I am a cruise ship entertainer. I juggle flaming torches in my act."

"Really," said the doubtful cop. "Well, lets see you do it."

So he got out and started juggling the blazing torches. As he was doing this, another car drove past them. The fellow behind the wheel turned to his wife and said, "I sure am glad I quit drinking. Look at the test they're giving now!"

An over-the-hill celebrity was doing a show on a cruise ship. He looked at the older crowd and said, "Hey, does anybody here remember who I am? Hunh?"

A fellow in the audience said, "No, but don't worry. Just go down to the front desk and they'll tell you."

What's the difference between a cruise ship musician and a large pizza?

A large pizza can feed a family of four.

What's the difference between a cruise ship musician and a government bond?

Eventually a government bond matures.

What do you call a cruise ship musician without a girlfriend?

Homeless.

After watching the band on his first cruise, seven-year-old Danny says to his dad, "I wanna grow up and be a musician!"

His dad says, "I'm sorry, son, you can't have it both ways."

"You can always tell the singers with the biggest egos. They're the ones who warm up by singing, "Me, me, mee ..."

A passenger walks into the lounge and asks the bartender, "How late does the band play?"

The bartender says, "About half a beat behind the drummer.

One night, the production show was terrible. The singers were off key, the orchestra was out of tune, and the dancers were falling over themselves. Everything was going wrong.

At a certain point, so many people were walking out, the Cruise Director yelled, "Wait! Women and children first!"

A guy and his wife are walking past the pianist in the ship's lobby. He says, "What's that guy playing?"

She says, "I think it's Chopin's Polonaise in A-flat."

"Oh," he says "I thought it was a piano."

A cruise ship comic came home late one night to find police cars and fire engines outside his house.

"I'm afraid I've got bad news," said one of the cops. "While you were out, your agent came to your home, kidnapped your family and burned down your house."

"I can't believe it," said the stunned comic. "My agent came to the house?"

The Cruise Director and a passenger were kidnapped by rebels while in Columbia. The rebels decided to shoot them, but before they did, they granted them each one last request.

The rebel leader asked the passenger, "What about you?"

The passenger replied, "Yes, I do have one. I've always loved "The Macarena." Could we do "The Macarena" one last time?"

The rebel leader agreed. Then he said to the Cruise Director, "What about you? What is your final request?"

The Cruise Director said, "Please, could you kill me first."

A ventriloquist is working on a cruise ship. In the middle of his show, a guy stands up and yells, "You've been making fun of how dumb us passengers are all night. Cut it out!"

The ventriloquist says, "Take it easy, pal. They're just jokes."

The guys says, "I'm not talking to you. I'm talking to the little guy on your knee!"

How many cruise ship audience members does it take to change a light bulb?

Two. One to do it and one to say, "Rose, they're changing the light bulb."

A guy sees a musician standing on the pier. He says, "How do you get on the cruise ship?"

The musician says, "Stop practicing."

Why was it so hard for the bandleader to write a drinking song?

He couldn't get past the first few bars.

This young Scottish musician got his first job on a cruise ship. After the first week, he phoned home to his mother.

"How's it going out there, son?" she asked.

"Fine Mother," he said, "but the people who live on these ships are very strange. The woman in the cabin next door cries all night long, and the fellow who lives on the other side of me is always banging on the walls."

"Well, I suggest that you do not associate with those kind of people," said his mother.

"I don't Mother," he said. "I just stay in my cabin all night, playing my bagpipes."

"Thank you. Thank you very much," said the ship's singer, after taking his bow. "You know, two years ago I had my voice insured with Lloyd's of London for $150,000."

"Really?" said a little old lady in the audience. "And what did you do with all the money?"

After a poorly attended performance, the guest entertainer called the Cruise Director and asked, "Didn't you tell the passengers that I was going to be performing?"

"No," said the cruise director, "but word must've leaked out."

An agent sent a tape to the talent coordinator at a cruise line, insisting he listen to it. When the talent coordinator played the tape, he was amazed.

"That was fabulous!" he said. "Is this singer your client?"

"No," said the agent, "that's Frank Sinatra ... but my client sounds just like him!"

This cruise ship entertainer ended his show by singing "I Left My Heart In San Francisco." During the song, he noticed a woman in the front row with tears in her eyes.

After the show, he asked, "Are you a San Franciscan?"

"No," she said, "I'm a music teacher."

MUTINY
ON THE BOUNTY

This pirate ship was sailing along one day when they came across an enemy warship.

The first mate reports to the captain, "Sir, an enemy vessel has been sighted on the horizon!"

The captain turns to his cabin boy and says, "Bring me my red shirt. If I'm wearing my red shirt and I'm wounded in battle, the men won't see the blood and will continue to fight!"

A few minutes later, the first mate returns, "Sir, there are now three enemy vessels on the horizon!"

The captain says, "Bring me my red shirt. If I'm wearing my red shirt and I'm wounded in battle, the men won't see the blood and will continue to fight!"

A few minutes later, the first mate returns, "Sir, there's now an entire fleet of enemy vessels! We're completely surrounded!"

The captain says, "Bring me my brown pants."

The Captain is out on deck one day when this guy comes by and asks him, "Are you a real sailor?"

"Well," says the Captain, "I spend my whole day thinking about sailing. When I get up in the morning, I think about sailing. When I go to bed at night, I think about sailing. So yes, I guess I'm a real sailor."

Later, a woman stops and asks him, "Are you a real sailor?"

"Well," says the Captain, "I spend my whole day thinking about sailing. When I get up in the morning, I think about sailing. When I go to bed at night, I think about sailing. So I guess I'm a real sailor. What about you?"

The woman says, "I'm a lesbian. I spend my whole day thinking about women. When I get up in the morning, I think about women. When I go to bed at night, I think about women. All I ever think about is women."

A little while later, another guy comes by and asks him, "Are you a real sailor?"

"Well," says the Captain, "up until about 10 minutes ago, I thought I was."

How can you tell a fax has been sent by the Captain?
There's a stamp on it.

How do you make the Captain laugh on Friday?
Tell him a joke on Monday.

"By the way, Captain," asked a passenger, "About how many crewmembers work onboard?"
"About half of them," replied the Captain.

The Captain, the First Mate and the Cruise Director were all kidnapped in Columbia. None of them had any family and couldn't be ransomed, so their captors decided to shoot them.

The kidnappers aimed their rifles at the Cruise Director. Suddenly, he yelled, "Flood!" Confused, his captors looked around to see where the flood was and he escaped.

The kidnappers aimed their rifles at the First Mate. He shouted, "Avalanche!" And when they looked around for the avalanche, he disappeared as well.

Seeing this, the Captain knew what to do. When they turned to aim their rifles at him, he yelled, "Fire!"

The Captain returned from port in a good mood and called the whole staff in to listen to a couple of jokes he had picked up.

Everybody laughed uproariously, except for one girl.

"What's the matter?" asked the Captain. "Don't you have a sense of humor?"

"I don't have to laugh," she said. "I'm signing off tomorrow."

One pitch black night, the Captain sees a light, dead ahead, on a collision course with his ship.

He sends a signal, "Change your course ten degrees west."

The light signals back, "Change your course ten degrees west."

The Captain signals back, "I am a cruise ship captain! You change your course!"

The light signals back, "I'm a seaman, second class. You change your course."

The Captain is furious, "This is a 90,000 ton cruise ship!"

The reply comes back, "This is a lighthouse."

The Captain goes up to the new social hostess and says, "There's a crew party tonight. Would you like to go?"

She says, "Great. It sounds like a nice way to meet some of my co-workers."

"Yes," says the Captain, "but I got to warn you. I've seen a lot of drinking at these things."

"That's okay," she says, "I enjoy a drink myself."

"And sometimes these things can get pretty rowdy as well."

"Oh, don't worry," she says, "I can take care of myself."

"And I seen a lot wild sex at these things."

"That's okay," she says, "I'm no prude."

"Alright then," says the Captain, " I'll see you at eight."

"Great," she says. "By the way, what should I wear?"

"Whatever you want. It's just going to be the two of us."

Two crew members meet in port one day. One says to the other, "Sometimes our Captain talks to himself. Does yours?"

"Yes, but he doesn't realize it. He thinks we're listening."

A new deckhand was given the job of varnishing the railing on the promenade deck.

"Start here," said the Captain, setting down the bucket of varnish, "and work your way around the ship."

The first day, the deckhand completed about 300 feet. The second day, 200 feet. The third day, less than 100 feet.

When the Captain noticed this, he said, "You're doing less and less work each day. What seems to be the problem?"

"It's not my fault," said the deckhand, "Everyday I get further and further away from the bucket!"

A young man was applying for a position on a cruise ship. Since there were several applicants and only one opening, everyone was required to take a test to see who was the most qualified for the job.

After reviewing the tests, the personnel manager took the young man aside and said, "Thank you for your interest but we've decided to give another man the job. Although you both missed only one question on the test, we feel the other fellow is more qualified."

"But if we both missed the same question, "asked the young man, "why give him the job?"

"Well, for one thing," said the personnel director, "on the question you both missed, he put down 'I don't know,' and you put down 'Neither do I?'"

"Old Sea Captains never die. They just keel over."

A crewman gets drunk one night and decides to call up his girlfriend. He misdials and ends up waking the Captain who says, "What do you think you're doing calling people at this hour of the night?"

The crewman says, "None of your business, you stupid jerk!"

The Captain says, "Do you know who I am? I'm the Captain of this vessel! You can't talk to me like that!"

The crewman says, "Well, do you know who I am?"

The Captain says, "No."

The crewman says, "Good."

And he hangs up.

Before going ashore for the day, the Captain tells his new deckhand to paint the railing of the ship.

Later that afternoon, when the Captain returns to the ship, he notices the distinctive smell of paint. He looks around for the new deckhand and finds him lying, unconscious, on the deck. The little man is wearing a parka and a wool jacket and is obviously suffering from heatstroke.

The Captain revives him and says, "What do you think you are you doing?"

"I'm painting the hull like you asked me too."

"But it's ninety degrees out here!" says the Captain. "Why on earth are you dressed like that?"

"Don't ask me," replies the deckhand. "The directions on the paint can said, 'For best results, put on two coats!'"

This guy is in the dining room with his fiancé, when he sees the Captain standing by the entrance. He excuses himself and goes over to talk with him.

"Excuse me, sir," he says, "my name is Bill. This is really a great honor to meet you. I was wondering if you could do me a big favor. I'm here with my fiancé and I'd like to make a good impression. If you could take a minute and come by our table and let me introduce you, I think she'd really be impressed."

The Captain agrees and Bill goes back to his table.

A few minutes later, the Captain walks over and says, "Hi there, Bill. It's great to see you. Would you mind introducing me to your lovely fiancé?"

Bill looks up and says, "Captain please, can you come back later? Can't you see we're trying to eat?"

A retired cruise ship Captain goes to his doctor for his annual checkup. The doctor says, "Any complaints?"

He says, "Well, my sex life ain't what it used to be."

"Really?" says the doctor. "When's the last time you had sex?"

"1950."

"Well, no wonder," says the doctor, "that's an awfully long time ago!"

"Oh, I don't know," says the Captain, looking at his watch. "It's only a little after 2100 right now."

The president of a major cruise line had a son who wanted to follow in his father's footsteps. Since the father started at the bottom, he felt his son should too. So he sent the young man out to work on one of the fleet's ships.

On his first day, the Head Housekeeper handed the young man a broom and told him to sweep the floor.

The young man looked at him with disgust and said, "I'll have you know that I'm a graduate of Harvard Law School."

"Oh, I'm sorry," said Head Housekeeper. "Here. Let me show you how it's done."

On his first day at sea, the new crewman goes to the crew office for his orientation lecture. The safety officer says, "We don't allow any fraternizing with the female crew members onboard. Your first infraction is a twenty-five dollar fine. Your second infraction is fifty dollars. And your third infraction will cost you one hundred dollars. Is that clear?"

"Fair enough," says the new crewman, pulling out his wallet. "How much for a season pass?"

Two new crewmen, Jorges and Ernesto, are given the job of scraping the hull. While they are toiling day after day in the hot sun, they can see the Captain is up in his air-conditioned office, relaxing. One day, Jorges says, "Why is he up there and we're down here?"

"I dunno," says Ernesto. "Maybe you should ask him."

So Jorges goes up to the bridge and asks, "Sir, my friend and I work all day long, scraping the deck in the hot sun. And you just walk around doing nothing? Why is that?"

The Captain says, "Because I'm smarter than you."

"Hunh?"

"I'll show you," he says. Then he holds his hand in front of a steel bulkhead and says. "See my hand? Go ahead and punch it as hard as you can."

Jorges punches as hard as he can. Just at the last second, the Captain pulls his hand away. Jorges ends up smashing his fish into the bulkhead.

"That's why I'm in charge," says the Captain. "Smarts."

Jorges nods and then he returns to his friend, nursing his bruised knuckles.

"What did the Captain tell you, Jorges?"

Jorges says, "It's all about smarts!"

"Smarts?"

"I'll show you," he says. Then he holds his hand in front of his face, "See my hand?"

What's the best way to get your cabin steward to bring you more towels?

Ask for more pillows.

A passenger was talking with his East Indian cabin steward. He said, "I've heard that, where you come from, a man doesn't even know his wife until he marries her. Is that really true?"

"Yes sir," said the cabin steward, "but I believe that is true in almost every country."

The cabin steward goes to the cabin of a retired English teacher and says, "I'm sorry, ma'am, but I don't got no towels. I bring them later."

"Young man," she says, "you mean, you don't have any towels. I don't have any towels. They don't have any towels. We don't have any towels. Do you see what I'm getting at?"

"I think so," says the cabin steward. "But what happen to all the towels?"

"My cabin steward is getting out of hand. This morning he made my bed while I was still in it."

A young blonde got a job on a cruise ship. On her first day, she was chatting with a passenger from New Zealand.

"New Zealand?" she said. "Where exactly is New Zealand?"

The fellow said, "If you know where Australia is — it's just a little bit further than that?"

"My goodness," she said, "you've certainly come a long way. How long have you been here?"

"Just a couple of days."

"Really?" she said. "Well, you've certainly picked up the language quickly enough."

Three new crewmembers join the ship. One is Italian, one is Greek and the other is Japanese.

The Food Manager takes them into the galley. He puts the Italian guy in charge of baking. He puts the Greek guy in charge of cleaning up. And he tells the Japanese fellow, "You'll be in charge of supplies."

The next morning, the three guys go to work, but at the end of the day, no one can find the Japanese crewmember.

They search the ship for hours. Finally, just as they are about to give up, the Japanese crewman jumps out from behind a counter and yells, "Supplies! Supplies!"

"Old sailors never die.
They just get a little dinghy."

How many cruise ship electricians does it take to change a light bulb?

Three. Two to hold the ladder and one to screw the bulb into the faucet.

On a particularly rocky day at sea, a new member of the cruise staff became extremely queasy due to seasickness. She headed for the restroom, but she was too late.

As she was making her way along the promenade deck, she could hold it in no longer, and threw up in the lap of a passenger who was dozing in one of the deck chairs.

When the fellow awoke, he was shocked to find himself covered in vomit. Thinking quickly, she looked down at him, smiled, and said, "There now. Are you feeling better?"

This cabin steward had a terrible stutter. One day, he ran up to the captain and said, "S-s-s-s-s-s-s-sir-sir-sir …"

The Captain said, "I'm a busy man. I don't have time for this. Whatever it is, you need to talk with the first mate."

So the cabin steward ran off to find the first mate. When he found him, he said, "S-s-s-s-s-s-s-s-s-sir-sir-sir …"

The First Mate said, "I'm too busy for this. You need to talk with your supervisor."

So the cabin steward ran off to find his supervisor. He said, "S-s-s-s-s-s-s-s-s-sir-sir-sir …"

His supervisor said, "Hold on a second. I've heard that people who stutter can sometimes communicate better if they sing. Why don't you try that?"

So the cabin steward sang:

"Should old acquaintance be forgot
And never brought to mind.
A passenger fell overboard
And he's twenty miles behind."

The guest lecturer was ill, so the Cruise Director asked the ship's doctor to fill in for him. When the doctor found out the topic that evening was sex, he was a bit embarrassed. So he told his wife that he would be talking about sailing instead.

The next day, one of the passengers ran into his wife and said, "Your husband's lecture last night was very informative. He brought a very unique perspective to the topic."

"I'm surprised to hear you say that," replied his wife. "I mean, he's only done it twice. The first time he threw up, and the second time, his hat blew off."

One day, the Cruise Director saw this attractive widow who was flirting with a member of the cruise staff.

The Cruise Director took the young man aside and said, "Bill, you're new here, so let me explain the rules. You are not allowed to fraternize with the guests. If you get caught, you could lose your job."

Bill said, "Oh, I wouldn't dream of such a thing, sir."

Several months passed. Then one day, the Cruise Director received a letter from an attorney. When he finished reading it, he called Bill into his office and said, "Bill, do you happen to remember that attractive widow who was flirting with you a few months back?"

"Yes sir, I do."

"And do you remember me warning you about fraternizing with the guests?"

"Yes sir, I do."

"And did you happen to disregard our little talk?"

"I'm sorry, sir, but I did."

"And did you happen to use my name instead of telling her your name?"

"I'm sorry, sir, but I did. Why do you ask?"

"Well, she just died and left me everything."

Being a security officer on a cruise ship is a difficult job. As the passengers are valued guests, a ship's security officer has to be firm and yet tactful.

One recruit was asked during his interview, "What would you do if you had to arrest your own mother?"

He said, "Call for backup."

A guest called the dining room and ordered a special cake for his wife's birthday celebration that night. In broken English, the chef asked what message he would like on the cake.

"Well," said the guest, "just put 'You're not getting older' at the top and 'You're getting better' at the bottom."

That evening, the cake showed up with this message:

YOU'RE NOT GETTING OLDER
AT THE TOP
YOU'RE GETTING BETTER
AT THE BOTTOM

Since English is usually their second language, some new crew members have a tough time filling out there job applications.

One guy did fine with Name, Age and Address, but when he got to the column marked, "Salary Expected," he wrote, "Yes."

One cruise line decided to change its employment policy and only hire married men.

When the press found out about it, they called the Human Resource Manager and asked, "Why would you limit your employees to married men? Is it because you think women are too weak, or aren't up to the job?"

"Not at all," the Manager replied. "It is because married men are used to obeying orders, are accustomed to being shoved around, know how to keep their mouths shut, and don't pout when they're yelled at."

The Purser went into her office one morning and found the Captain standing next to the paper shredder with a piece of paper. She asked, "Can I help you, sir?"

He said, "Yes, I got a very important document here and I can't get this thing to work. Can you take care of it for me?"

"Certainly," said the Purser. Then she turned on the machine, pressed the start button and inserted the document.

"Great," said the Captain, as the paper disappeared into the machine. "I just need one copy."

The Captain was getting ready to go home for Christmas. He went into a pet shop in Fort Lauderdale to purchase something special for his wife.

"How about a Christmas Parrot?" said the shopkeeper.

"What's a Christmas Parrot?" asked the Captain.

The shopkeeper went in the back room and came out with a red and green parrot. He said, "This bird is very rare. He sings Christmas carols, but you got to warm him up first."

Then the shopkeeper took out a lighter and put it under the bird's left wing. The bird sang, "Silent Night." Then he put it under the bird's right wing and the bird sang, "Jingle Bells."

The Captain took the bird home to his wife and said, "Look what I bought for you. It's a Christmas Parrot. Watch this."

Then he lit a candle and put it under the bird's left wing. The bird sang, "Silent Night." He put it under the bird's right wing and it sang, "Jingle Bells."

His wife said, "That's incredible!"

Then she took the candle and put it under the bird's tail. The bird sang, "Chestnuts roasting on an open fire ..."

A sailor walked into a bar. He sat next to an old pirate who had a peg leg, a hook on one arm and an eye patch.

The sailor asked, "How did you get the peg leg?"

"Well," said the pirate, "I was shipwrecked and while I was floating out at sea, a shark came by and bit off my leg."

"And how did you get the hook?"

"Well," said the pirate, "I was in a sword fight one night and this fellow snuck up behind me and cut off my hand."

"And what about the eye patch?"

"I got that," said the pirate, "when this seagull flew over and pooped in my eye."

"I find that hard to believe," said the sailor. "How can you lose an eye from seagull poop?"

"Well, you see," said the pirate, "it was my first day with the hook."

Every week, the ship would dock in Juneau. While they were in port, the Captain would go to the Red Dog Saloon and hang out with the locals. One afternoon, he said to the bartender, "You know, I'm beginning to feel like a native Alaskan."

"Not even close," said the bartender. "You can't be a native here until you can down a pint of whiskey in one gulp, French kiss an Eskimo girl and shoot a Grizzly Bear."

So the Captain grabbed a pint of whiskey, slugged it down in one gulp, and headed out the door.

About an hour later, he staggered back in, a bloody mess, his clothes ripped to shreds.

"Okay," he said, looking around the bar, "Now where's that Eskimo girl I'm supposed to shoot?"

The first mate goes up to the Captain and says, "Sir, we've discovered a case of Meningitis onboard."

"Wonderful," says the Captain. "I was getting tired of the Chablis."

One day, a lady in the penthouse suite called the Purser's Desk to complain, "I called two days ago to have our doorbell fixed. Why haven't you sent anyone?"

"We did, ma'am," said the Purser. "The electrician came by yesterday. He rang three times, but nobody answered. So he figured you weren't in."

A Czechoslovakian waiter goes to the ship's doctor to have his eyes checked. The doctor points at the wall chart and asks him if he can read the bottom line.

The waiter looks at the chart and says, "The bottom line? Okay… H… L… K… V… C… Z… M... Hey, I know the guy!"

IN CASE OF
EMERGENCY - PANIC

What happened to the survivors when the red cruise ship collided with the blue cruise ship?

They were marooned.

What lies at the bottom of the ocean and twitches?

A nervous wreck.

What do you get when you cross the Atlantic Ocean with the Titanic?

Half-way.

Two retired accountants, Norman and Sidney were on the Titanic. As the ship sank, Sidney broke out in tears.

Norman turned to him and said, "Sidney, why are you so upset? It's not your boat?"

As the ship was leaving port, the Captain came on the public address system to welcome the passengers.

"Ladies and gentlemen, this is your captain speaking. Welcome aboard our seven day cruise to the Western Caribbean. The weather is good. We expect calm seas for the next few days. So relax and enjoy your yourselves in one of our many ... OH MY GOD!"

The ship lurched to starboard. There was silence for a few minutes as it righted itself. Then the captain came back on the intercom and said, "Ladies and Gentlemen, I wish to apologize if I scared you earlier, but while I was speaking, one of our waiters brought me a cup of coffee and spilled it in my lap. Boy, you should see the front of my pants!"

To which one of the passengers replied, "That's nothing. You should see the back of mine!"

Two blondes were stranded on an iceberg with only a telescope. As she was scanning the horizon, one blonde said to the other, "We're saved! Look, it's the Titanic!"

Three guys -- one Catholic, one Protestant and one Jewish -- find themselves marooned on a deserted island.

The Catholic kneels down and prays for God to deliver them.

The Protestant sings a hymn, then bows his head and prays for God to deliver them.

The Jewish guy looks at the others and says, "Relax, fellas. Two years ago, I gave a million dollars to the Jewish Federation. Last year, I gave then two million. And this year, I pledged three million dollars. Don't worry, they'll find me."

This guy was left stranded alone on a deserted island with nothing but coconuts and bananas.

One day, he spotted a outrigger canoe, and in it was the most beautiful woman he'd ever seen.

In disbelief, he asked her, "Where did you come from? How did you get here?"

She said, "I live on the other side of the island. I was stranded here when my ship sank."

He said, "I didn't know anyone else had survived,"

"I'm afraid it's only the two of us," she said. "I've been here for months with no one to talk to, and no food or supplies."

"Then how did you get the outrigger?" he asked.

"Oh, simple," she said. "I made the it out of materials I found on the island."

"That's amazing," stuttered the man. "You did that with no tools or hardware. How did you manage?"

"That was no big deal," she said. "I used rocks and coral to make the tools, and the tools to make the hardware."

While the woman anchored the canoe with an expertly woven rope, the man could only stare, dumbstruck.

Then she unloaded a large gourd and two hollowed out coconut shells and said casually, "Would you like a drink?"

"No thanks," he said. "I'm sick of coconut juice."

"It's not coconut juice," the woman replied. "I have a still. How about a Pina Colada?"

She poured him a drink. Then she leaned in seductively and said, "It must have been lonely out her all this time. Is there something you've been longing for all these months?"

"You mean?" he replied, "I can check my e-mail from here?"

One afternoon, the ship had to delay their departure from port because three crew members showed up late.

That evening, they were ordered to report to the captain's quarters to explain their actions. The captain called in the first crewman. He said, "You were late returning to the ship. That's a serious offense. What do you have to say for yourself?"

"Well sir," said the crewman, "it was like this. I went to town and found a little pub where I could share a few drinks with the locals. After awhile, I looked at my watch and noticed it was getting late. So I went outside to hire a taxi. But there weren't any. So I hired a horse and buggy instead. We headed back to the ship. We went down a big hill and up a big hill, but the strain was too much for the horse and he died."

The captain said, "That sounds like a reasonable explanation. Send the next man in."

The second crewman came in. The captain said, "You were late returning to the ship. What's your explanation?"

The second crewman said, "Well sir, it was like this. I went to town and found a little pub where I could share a few drinks with the locals. After awhile, I looked at my watch and noticed it was getting late. So I went outside to hire a taxi. But there weren't any. So I hired a horse and buggy instead. We headed back to the ship. We went down a big hill and up a big hill, but the strain was too much for the horse and he died."

"Amazing," said the captain, "I heard a story like that not two minutes ago. I guess it's possible. Send the next man in."

The third crewman came in. The captain said, "You were late returning to the ship. What's your explanation?"

The third crewman said, "Well sir, it was like this ..."

"Wait just a minute," said the captain. "Why don't I tell you what happened?"

"Certainly sir." said the crewman.

"You went to town and found a little pub where you could share a few drinks with the locals."

"I did."

"And after awhile, you looked at your watch and noticed it was getting late."

"I did."

"So you went outside to hire a taxi."

"I did."

"But there weren't any."

"No sir, there were!"

"There were?"

"Yes, lots of them. I hopped in the first one I saw. We headed back to the ship. We went down a big hill and up a big hill, but we couldn't get through for all the dead horses."

A philosophy professor and his friend were stranded on a deserted island. One day they saw an old bottle on the beach. When the professor picked it up, a genie appeared.

"I'll grant you one wish," said the genie. "You can either have infinite wisdom or infinite wealth. Which do you choose?"

The professor said, "I'll take infinite wisdom."

There was a puff of smoke. When it cleared, the professor stood on the beach, a faint halo glowing around his head.

His friend said, "Say something."

The professor thought for a moment and said, "I should have taken the money."

Another guy was stranded on a deserted island. He had been there for months, surviving on nothing but fish and coconuts.

One day, to his surprise, a scuba diver appeared in the lagoon. When he ran down to the beach, he realized the diver was a beautiful woman.

"I've been stranded for months," he cried. "Thank god you've come."

"How long has it been since you've had a smoke." asked the woman, as she unzipped a waterproof pocket on her sleeve and pulled out a pack of cigarettes.

"Oh, that's great," said the guy, puffing deeply. "I haven't had one of these in months."

"And how long since you've had a good, stiff drink?" asked the woman as she unzipped a waterproof pocket on her ankle and pulled out a flask.

"Oh man, this is great!" said the man, slugging down a big gulp. "I really needed that."

"And how long has it been since you had some real fun?" asked the woman, as she began unzipping the front of her wetsuit.

"Oh my gosh!" said the man, barely able to contain his excitement. "Don't tell me you got a set of golf clubs in there!"

As the ship passed slowly by a small island, the passengers were fascinated by the sight of a bedraggled, bearded man on the beach, desperately shouting and waving his arms.

One of them asked the Captain, "Who is that guy?"

"I have no idea," replied the Captain, shaking his head, "but every year when we pass that island, he goes crazy."

Three guys were trapped on a deserted island.

One day, a bottle washed up on shore. When they pulled the cork, a genie appeared and offered each guy one wish.

The first guy said, "It's awful lonely here without my family. I wish I was home with them."

Poof!

The guy disappeared from the island and was immediately transported to his family's home.

The second guy said, "It's awfully lonely here without my wife and daughter. I wish I was home with them."

Poof!

He also disappeared from the island and was immediately transported back to his wife and baby.

The third guy thought for a little bit and said, "It sure is lonely on this island without anybody to talk to. I sure wish my two buddies were back here with me."

Poof!

A woman fell overboard on a New England cruise. Several days later, a local fisherman discovered her body and contacted her distraught husband.

"I got good news and bad news," said the fisherman.

"What's the bad news?" said the husband.

"Your wife is definitely deceased. When we pulled her up out of the water, she had two large lobsters and several edible crabs on her." said the fisherman.

"That's terrible," said the husband. "What could possibly be the good news?"

"We're going to pull her up again tomorrow?"

One night there was a fire onboard. It was spreading rapidly and the captain sounded the alarm to abandon ship.

Standing at the railing, a man yelled to his wife, "Jump!"

"I can't!" she cried. "We're on the thirteenth floor!"

"Oh, for heaven's sake!" he hollered back. "This is no time to be superstitious!"

A preacher was on a cruise when his ship hit an iceberg and sank. As he was floating in the frigid water, he prayed for God to save him. Suddenly he heard a booming voice say, "The Lord will provide."

A while later, a rescue boat came by.

"Get in," yelled the captain, "we've come to save you."

"Don't worry about me," replied the preacher. "The Lord will provide."

An hour later, a helicopter dropped a rope. The pilot yelled, "Grab on! We'll save you!"

"Don't worry about me," replied the preacher, waving them off. "The Lord will provide!"

A little later, a seaplane landed, and a rescue worker called out, "Hey buddy, get in the plane. This is your last chance."

"Oh, don't worry about me," said the preacher. "The Lord will provide."

Two days later, the preacher finally drowned. When he arrived at the Pearly Gates, he was furious.

"What's the deal?" he said. "I thought the Lord was going to provide!"

"What do you want?" came the thunderous reply. "I sent a boat. I sent a plane. I sent a helicopter."

LIFE'S
A BEACH

A lady is playing on the beach with her grandson. All of a sudden, this enormous wave crashes on the shore and pulls the child out to sea.

The lady looks up to the heavens and says, "Lord, Lord, I beg of you. Please return my grandson to me!"

When the next wave comes in, it drops her grandson on the shore right where he had been sitting before.

The lady looks up and says, "He had a hat."

Ben and Jerry went on a fishing excursion in Mazatlan and came back with three tiny fish.

Ben looked over their catch and said, "The way I figure it, each one of these fish cost us over $200."

"Well then," said Jerry, "it's a good thing we didn't catch any more of them that we did."

What's the scariest sight to see from the new glass bottom boat?
  The old glass bottom boat.

Several tourists were on a dive boat in the middle of the ocean. Everything was going fine until the boat sprung a leak and started to sink. The guide thought for a moment and said, "Okay fellas, for $25 extra you guys get to do a wreck dive!"

Name three reasons scuba divers always dive with a buddy?
  1) If you run out of air, your buddy can help you.
  2) If you have a problem, your buddy can help you.
  3) If you see a shark, the odds are 50-50, instead of 100%."

What has two sets of gills and one leg?
  A shark with his mouth full.

What do you call a man with a seagull on his head?
  Cliff.

What did one ocean say to the other ocean?
  Nothing. They just waved.

A fellow goes into a dive shop in the Bahamas, hands the owner his credit card and says, "I'd like to rent some equipment. I'm going to dive with the sharks."
  The owner says, "You ever with the sharks before?"
  "No," says the tourist. "This will be my first time."
  "Well then," says the owner, "I am afraid I'm going to have to ask you to pay cash."

Jimmy returned to the ship after a deep-sea fishing excursion with his dad. The youth counselor noticed the little boy was crying, so he went over and said, "What's the matter, Jimmy?"

Jimmy said, "My dad and I went out fishing and he caught the biggest marlin you've ever seen. He fought that fish for hours and just as he was about to reel it into the boat, the line snapped and it got away."

The youth counselor said, "A big boy like you shouldn't cry over something like that. You should have just laughed it off."

"But that's just what I did."

How much do pirates pay for their earrings?

A buccaneer.

A woman was standing in front of the counter at a jewelry store when she start praying at the top of her lungs, "Dear Lord! I would love to have this diamond necklace for my birthday!"

"Why are you yelling?" asked the clerk. "God isn't deaf."

"I know," said the woman, "but my husband is."

VINI, VIDI, VISA
I came, I saw, I shopped.

Two husbands were sitting outside one of the many gift shops in port. One turned the other and said, "I had my credit card stolen awhile ago."

The other guy said, "Really? Did you report it?"

"I was going to," said the first guy, "but so far, the thief is spending less than my wife."

After two weeks of Five Star service, Leslie and June were getting a little too used to being pampered.

As the ship dropped anchor in Fiji, Leslie said, "I am really looking forward to seeing these islands. I've heard there are some beaches where precious gems are just lying in the sand. All you have to do is bend over and pick them up."

June said, "Bend over?"

"The port talks are educational. Whenever they have one, I go to my cabin and read a book."

An elderly couple were checking out the brochures at the shore excursion desk.

The husband asked, "How much is the helicopter tour?"

The girl at the counter said, "Three hundred dollars."

"Three hundred dollars," the guy said to his wife. "That seems like an awful lot of money just to look around a helicopter."

After a stop in The Netherlands, the tour guide came back to the ship. He went to a woman's cabin and knocked on her door.

"I'm sorry to have to tell you this, ma'am," he said, "but there was an accident on the tour of the beer factory."

"Oh no!" she cried, "Please don't tell me ..."

"I'm sorry," said the guide, "but your husband fell into a vat of beer and drowned."

"Was it was quick?" she asked.

"Well, not exactly," said the tour guide. "As a matter of fact, he got out three times to use the bathroom."

One of the passengers showed up for dinner, bruised and battered, and with a big lump on his head.

A lady at his table said, "What happened to you?"

He said, "I went horseback riding this afternoon and it was just awful. I lost control of the horse and when he threw me off, I got my foot caught in the stirrups. I was dragged along behind and wretched horse refused to stop or even slow down. I would have been killed if the manager at Walmart hadn't come out and unplugged the machine."

"I'm not lost. I'm discovering alternative destinations."

After years of service, Sister Mary Margaret and Sister Agnes were given a two week vacation, so they went on a cruise to the Caribbean. They rented a car in Nassau to see the sights, but they got lost and ended up in a seedy part of town. When they stopped to ask directions, they were accosted by a drunk who staggered up and hopped on the hood of their car.

Mary Margaret tapped gently on the window, but the man ignored her. So Sister Agnes suggested, "Perhaps you could try reasoning with the man — explain our situation?"

So Mary Margaret rolled down the window and said, "Sir, please, we are two poor nuns on our first vacation in years. If you don't get let us go, we will miss our transportation home."

Still, the man ignored her. So Sister Agnes said, "Perhaps you could try showing him your cross?"

"That's a good idea," said Mary Margaret. She leaned out the window and said, "GET THE @#$% OFF OUR CAR!"

A tourist rents a car to see the sights. He gets in a collision with one of the local cab drivers. While they're surveying the damage, the cabbie asks him how he's feeling.

The guy says, "I'm a little shaken up, actually."

The cabbie hands him a flask and says, "Here, this will help settle your nerves."

The guy thanks him and takes a big swig. Then he hands back the flask and says, "Here, you have one too."

The cabbie says, "Oh, I'd rather not. The police should be here any minute."

This guy gets jumped in an alleyway while he's sightseeing. He puts up a tremendous struggle, but eventually the two men overpower him. When they go through his pockets, they are surprised to only find a few coins.

One of the muggers says, "I can't believe someone would put up such a fight for a lousy 83 cents!"

The guy looks up and says, "I didn't. I thought you were after the three hundred bucks in my shoe."

A tourist hops in a cab in Barbados. After a few minutes, he notices the driver is going the wrong way, so he reaches forward and taps the him on the shoulder.

The cabby freaks out and starts screaming wildly. The car goes out of control and runs off the road into a ditch.

After things settle down, the tourist says, "Sorry about that. I didn't realize you were so skittish."

The driver says, "That's okay, man. It's my first day on the job. For the last 10 years, I was driving a hearse."

A peasant approached a passing tourist and said, "Excuse me, sir, I was wondering if you could give a few dollars to help out this poor family in our village. The father is dead, the mother is too sick to work, the children are hungry, and the whole family is about to be thrown out into the street unless they can collect enough money to pay their rent."

"How sad," said the tourist. "Are you a friend of theirs?"

"No," said the peasant, "I'm their landlord."

A lady was waiting in line to get on the tour bus to go sightseeing. When it was her turn to get on the bus, she became aware that with all the food she had been eating all week, her skirt was too tight to allow her leg to come up to the height of the first step.

So, slightly embarrassed, and with a quick smile to the bus driver, she reached behind her and unzipped her skirt a little, hoping to give her enough slack to raise her leg.

She tried a second time, but still couldn't make the step. So, slightly more embarrassed, she reached behind her and unzipped her skirt a little more.

She tried again, but still couldn't raise her leg to the step. So, she reached back and unzipped her skirt a little more.

At this point, the guy in line behind her placed his hand on her backside and pushed her up onto the bus.

The woman turned around and screeched at him, "How dare you touch my body! I don't even know you!"

"Well, ma'am," the guy said, softly, "normally I would agree with you. But after you unzipped my fly for the third time, I kind of figured we were friends."

Three tourists were hiking through the Alaska woods when they came across some tracks.

The first guy said, "These are deer tracks."

The second guy said, "No, they're moose tracks."

The third guy said, "No, they're elk tracks."

They were still arguing when the train ran them over.

"I don't understand Alaskan cruises. Who saves up all winter just so they can go and watch ice melt?"

A tourist runs up to the conductor, standing under a huge sign that reads: Yukon Scenic Rail Excursion.

He says, "Excuse me, does this train go to the Yukon?"

The conductor says, "No, this train goes toot toot."

During mating season, the Alaskan Grizzly can be especially dangerous. Last year, a female passenger was, not only attacked, but actually molested by one of these ferocious animals.

A few months after the incident, she was interviewed by a reporter who inquired how she was doing after the attack.

"How do you think I'm doing?" she said, wiping away a tear, "He hasn't called, he hasn't written ... "

Before docking in Juneau, the ship's naturalist warned a passenger, "If you happen to stumble on a bear, try not to act afraid. Bears can smell fear."

The passenger said, "Oh don't worry. If I stumble on a bear, he's going to smell a lot more than just fear."

Edna was looking around the gift shops in Juneau when she saw a teddy bear dressed in a sailor outfit. Since her husband was a retired Navy Captain, she thought it would be a cute idea to bring the toy home for her four-year-old grandson, Timmy.

Later, when Timmy opened his present, Edna said, "This is what your Grandpa used to be before you were born."

"Really?" said Timmy. "Grandpa used to be a bear?"

The ship's naturalist was giving a talk on Alaskan wildlife. He said, "You need to be especially careful of bears. They can be very dangerous. Last year I came across a 1200 pound Grizzly Bear up here. They say in the guide books you're supposed to stand perfectly still, but it didn't work. This bear just reared up on his haunches and let loose this deafening roar and started charging. Fortunately, just inches away from me, he slipped and tumbled down the side of the mountain."

Some guy in the audience said, "Wow, if that happened to me, I would have soiled my pants!"

The naturalist said, "Well, what do you think he slipped on?"

The Shore-Excursion Manager sent a newlywed couple off on a fishing trip in Alaska. When he ran into the young bride later that day, he said, "So how was the first fishing trip with that new husband of yours?"

She said, "Oh, everything went wrong. First, he said I was talking too loud and I was going to scare the fish. Then he said I was using the wrong bait. Then I wasn't putting it on the hook right. Then I was reeling in too fast. And then, to make matters worse, I ended up catching the most fish!"

A cop pulls over three lady tourists going 20 miles an hour in a rental car. He walks up to the driver's side window and says, "Excuse me, ma'am, but this is a 65 mile per hour highway. Why are you going so slow?"

The driver says, "But officer, the sign said 22, not 65."

"Oh, that's not the speed limit," says the cop, "that's the name of the highway you're on!"

"Oh, silly me!" she says, "from now on, I'll be more careful."

At this point, the cop looks in the backseat where the other ladies are shaking and trembling.

"Excuse me, ma'am," he says, "but what's wrong with your friends back there? They're shaking something terrible."

"Oh, we just got off of Highway 119."

TOUR GUIDE AT THE SAN DIEGO ZOO

"Ladies and gentlemen, this is the elephant, the largest animal to roam the lands. Every day the elephant eats three dozen bunches of bananas, six tons of hay, and two thousand pounds of fruit. Ma'am, please don't stand near the elephant's backside ... Please don't stand near the elephant's ... Too late. George, dig her out."

The ship's security officer saw a young lady walking up the gangway with her blouse unbuttoned and her breast exposed.

Not wanting to embarrass the woman, the security officer walked over and said quietly, "Excuse me, ma'am. I believe you've forgotten something."

The woman looked down, horrified, and cried, "Oh my god! I left the baby on the tour bus!"

A tour guide came back to the ship with a black eye.

"What happened to you?" asked the cruise director.

"Well, I was standing in line behind this rather large woman, waiting for the tour bus today," said the guide, "and I noticed her skirt was tucked into her backside. Now, I didn't want to embarrass her by calling attention to it. So I just tugged a bit on the back of her skirt to untuck it."

"And she hit you for that?" asked the cruise director.

"No," said the guide, "but she cussed me out pretty good."

"Then how did you get the black eye?"

"Well, when I saw how angry she got, I started thinking maybe she preferred it way it was. So I tucked it back in."

A guide at the San Diego Zoo was giving a tour of the elephant exhibit when one of the elephants farted so loudly it could not be ignored.

The guide said, "How embarrassing. I really must apologize."

"That's quite alright," said one of the tourists. "As a matter of fact, I thought it was the elephant."

A guide was taking some tourists on a walking tour when he said, "Oh look. A dead bird."

They all looked up and said, "Where?"

Two tourists are waiting at the bus stop.

When the bus pulls up and opens the door, the first one says, "Will this bus take me to the aquarium?"

The driver shakes his head and says, "Sorry, ma'am."

Then the second one smiles and says, "How about me?"

A drunk walks out of a bar in Miami and sees a woman with a poodle. The drunk says, "Hey, where did you get that pig?"

The woman looks at him and says, "I'll have you know, sir, this is a French poodle."

The drunk looks at her and says, "I'll have you know, ma'am, I was talking to the poodle."

A guy walks into a shop in Nassau and orders conk chowder. The shopkeeper says, "You want conk chowder? Oh, you must be one of those dumb tourists."

They guy says, "Why would you say that? Because I ordered conk chowder?"

"No, because this is a hardware store."

A tourist goes into a little bar in Key West and sees a dog sitting a chair, playing poker.

He says, "Is the dog really playing poker?"

"Yeah," says the bartender, "but he's really not that good. Whenever he has a good hand, he wags his tail."

After a day of sightseeing in Central America, this lady returns to the ship, carrying a monkey.

She shows the monkey to her cabin steward and says, "I just bought this little guy as a pet. My husband and I don't have any children, so I thought he could come home with us. He would be like one of the family. He could eat at our table. He could even sleep in the same bed with me and my husband."

The cabin steward says, "But what about the smell?"

"Well, he'll just have to get used to it, the same as I did."

While sightseeing near a small village in South America, a tourist was amazed to see a flock of three-legged chickens.

"These chickens are quite unusual looking," he said to one of the local farmers. "How do they taste?"

The farmer said, "I don't know. We've never caught one."

A sixty-year-old guy is walking along the beach with his wife when he comes across a magic lamp, lying in the sand. He rubs the lamp and a genie appears.

The genie says, "I'll grant you one wish."

The guy looks at his wife and says, "I want to be married to someone thirty years younger than me."

POOF! The guy is ninety-years-old.

Bill left the ship one morning to play a round of golf with his friend, Harry. That afternoon, he returned alone. His wife asked him what happened to Harry.

Bill said, "I couldn't believe it. On the third tee, Harry just dropped dead from a heart attack."

His wife said, "Oh, that's terrible."

Bill said, "You're telling me — all day long it was hit the ball, drag Harry, hit the ball, drag Harry …"

"Why don't you golf with your friend, Jeff, anymore?"

"Would you golf with a guy who constantly lies about his handicap, cheats on his score and makes distracting noises when you're trying to putt?"

"No, I wouldn't."

"Well, neither will Jeff."

A fellow went to the ship's golf pro and said, "I want to learn to play golf in the worst way."

"Well," said the golf pro, "you've already accomplished that. What else would you like to work on?"

"The other day I broke 70. That's a lot of clubs!"

The ship's golf pro died and was greeted by Saint Peter at the Pearly Gates. Saint Peter said, "You've led a good life. You were honest and caring and a good husband. But it says here that there was one time you took the Lord's name in vain."

"Let me explain," said the man. "It happened about a year ago. I was playing at our club tournament and I was doing beautifully. On the eighteenth hole, all I needed was an easy par four to win the trophy. My tee shot was long enough, but it landed in the rough."

"I see," said Saint Peter. "So is that when you took the Lord's name in vain?"

"No, no," said the guy. "I knew if I hit the ball just right, I could probably still reach the green. And I did, too. But then the ball rolled back and into a sand trap."

"Oh, I hate when that happens," said Saint Peter. "So that's when you took the Lord's name in vain?"

"Oh no," said the guy. "I was frustrated, but I kept my cool. I checked all the angles and took my time and when I took the shot, the ball ended up just a foot away from the cup."

"Oh no!" said Saint Peter. "Don't tell me you missed the goddamn putt!"

Jim came back to the ship after a day of golf, looking quite upset. When the bartender asked him what was wrong, Bill said, "I had a terrible day. I was on the fourteenth fairway when I sliced the ball clear out into the road. It went through a car windshield, causing the driver to swerve into the oncoming traffic. It was a horrible accident. There were cars piled up all over the place."

"That's terrible," said the bartender. "What did you do?"

"Well," said Jim, "I closed up on my stance and shortened my back swing a little."

On the first tee, this fellow was taking forever to hit the ball. Finally the golf pro says, "We haven't got all day."

The guy says, "Sorry, but my wife's standing over by the clubhouse there, and I want this to be a perfect shot."

The golf pro says, "Forget it. You'll never hit her from here."

Two strangers, Bill and Ted, get paired up on a golf excursion in St. Thomas. The day goes great until they get stuck behind two women who are playing very slow. Finally Bill turns to Fred and says, "Why don't you go up there and ask those ladies if we can play through."

Fred says okay and starts walking over to the ladies. A few minutes later, he comes back, shaking his head.

He says, "Sorry pal, but when I got up a little closer, I noticed one of those ladies is my wife and the other is my mistress. So I figured maybe you better talk to them instead."

Bill agrees and heads over to the ladies. A few minutes later, he comes back and says, "Small world, isn't it?"

Cliff diving is one of the most popular tourist attractions in Acapulco. Tourists come from all over the world to watch the local divers climb up the slippery cliff face and stand on the tiny diving platform, 200 feet above the ocean, watching the waves below, waiting for the perfect moment to dive — a moment too early or a moment too late and they will be crushed on the rocks below -- they take a breath, soar into space and plunge into the crashing surf.

One day, after this impressive stunt, one of the divers was approached by a tourist.

"That was really amazing," said the tourist. "I've never seen anyone so calm in the face of death. How did you end up in a job like this?"

"Well," said the diver, "I used to drive the school bus, but after awhile my nerves gave out."

"I'm a scratch golfer. I write down all my good scores and scratch out all the bad ones."

This guy is walking around Acapulco, looking at the sights, when a woman approaches him and says, "For fifty dollars, I'll do anything you want."

The guy pulls out a fifty and says, "Great! Paint my house."

"I'm taking my wife to Bali for our twentieth anniversary."

"That's going to be tough to beat. What are you going to do for your twenty-fifth?"

"Maybe I'll go back and get her."

This guy goes to watch the cliff divers in Acapulco. After they're done, he decides to climb up the rock face and see if he can get a picture from their diving perch.

When he gets to the top, he slips and falls over the edge. But fortunately, he grabs hold of a tiny bush growing out of the cliff. As he's hanging there, 200 feet above the rocks below, he yells out, "Is anybody up there?"

From above, he hears a deep voice say, "I'm here, my son. It's the Lord. Have faith. Let go of the bush and I will save you."

The guy looks up. The he looks down at the rocks. Then he looks up again and says, "Is there anybody else up there?"

A tourist rented a car in Jamaica, but he was worried that the turn indicator was burned out. He told his wife to go around to the back of the car and check it.

"Is it working?" he asked.

"Yes ... no ... yes ... no ... yes ... "

This lady takes a scenic flight excursion of Hawaii in a four engine plane. All of a sudden there's a loud bang. The pilot comes on the radio and says, "I'm sorry, folks, our first engine has gone out. Our landing will be delayed about 15 minutes."

Then there's another bang. Once again, the radio comes on and the pilot says the same thing except that the second engine shut down and that they'll be delayed nearly half an hour.

After that, the third engine shuts off and the pilot tells the passengers that they will be delayed more than an hour. The lady turns to the guy sitting beside her and says, "Man, if the fourth engine shuts off we'll be up here all day."

Dave and Myrna overslept on the day they were supposed to take a scenic flight excursion. They missed the bus, so they took a cab to the airfield. When they arrived, they saw a small plane warming up on the airstrip.

"We're in luck. The pilot waited for us," said Dave.

They ran to the plane. Myrna jumped in the back and Dave took the co-pilot's seat.

"Sorry, I'm late," he said to the pilot. "What do you say we get this baby up in the air?"

"Okay," said the pilot, and off they went. As the plane climbed into the air, Dave pulled out a map of some of the various points of interest and suggested, "Why don't we start by flying over the cruise ship? I want some photos to show everybody where we went on our vacation."

"Vacation?" said the wide-eyed pilot. "You mean you're not the instructor?"

"If at first you don't succeed, skydiving is definitely not for you."

A one-legged scuba diver goes to apply for an insurance policy. The agent asks him if he ever had any accidents, and the scuba diver says no.

The agent says, "Then what happened to your leg?"

The scuba diver says, "It got bitten off by a shark."

"Well, wouldn't you call that an accident?"

"No, he did it on purpose."

AROUND THE WORLD IN EIGHTY JOKES

The guy goes into the barber shop. He's all excited. He says, "I need a haircut. I'm going on a Mediterranean cruise. We're stopping in Rome and I might even get to meet the Pope."

His barber says, "Those Mediterranean cruises are terrible this time of year. Rome is nothing but a tourist trap, and if you actually see the Pope, it'll be with ten thousand other people and you'll probably be stuck in the back."

So the guy goes to Rome. When he gets back, his barber asks him, "How was it?"

The guy says, "It was great! It was a wonderful cruise. Rome was a beautiful city ... and I got to meet the Pope!"

"You actually met the Pope?"

"Sure did."

"What did he say?"

"He said, 'Where'd you get that lousy haircut?'"

While stopping in a small Italian port town, this American tourist noticed an unusual funeral procession. A young man with a dog on a leash was following a horse drawn casket, and behind him there were hundreds of men walking in single file.

As they passed by, the American asked what was going on.

The young man said, "It is my mother-in-law's funeral."

"Really," said the American, looking at the long procession of mourners. "She must have been very popular."

"Not at all," said the young man. "She was a hateful woman with a mean disposition and a sharp tongue. She was always criticizing and belittling me. Then one day, this dog attacked her and killed her."

The American said, "Do you mind if I borrow the dog."

"Not at all," said the young man. "Get in line."

When Barbara returned from her month long cruise to the Mediterranean, her friend asked, "How was your trip?"

"Just terrible!" said Barbara. "Everywhere we went was full of foreigners."

Two men are sightseeing at the Eiffel Tower when one of them is attacked by a Rottweiler.

Thinking quickly, the other man takes his umbrella, wedges it into the dog's collar and twists, breaking the dog's neck.

A local reporter sees the incident and writes in his notebook:
"BRAVE PARISIAN SAVES FRIEND FROM VISCIOUS ANIMAL"

The guy says, "I'm not from Paris. I'm visiting from America."

The reporter starts a new sheet in his notebook and writes,
"UGLY AMERICAN KILLS FAMILY PET."

On a tour of the Sistine Chapel, the guide explained that it took four years to paint the ceiling.

"Yeah," said one of the tourists, "I used to have a landlord like that myself."

A 10 pm curfew was imposed in Belfast. Everybody had to be off the streets or risk being shot.

On the first night of the curfew, a soldier shot one of the citizens at 9.45 pm. When asked why he opened fire, the soldier replied, "Well, I know where he lives and he never would have made it."

A group of Americans were cruising around Ireland. On a shore excursion to the site of the famous Blarney Stone, one of the women in the group was constantly complaining. The bus seats were uncomfortable. The food was bad. It was too hot. It was too cold. Everything was terrible.

When they got to the site, the local tour guide announced, "Legend has it that good luck will follow you all of your days if you kiss the Blarney Stone. Unfortunately, folks, it's being cleaned this afternoon and so no one will be able to kiss it. Perhaps you can wait till this evening?"

"We can't wait," the nasty woman shouted. "We're sailing at five and tomorrow we'll be at some other port. I paid to kiss that stupid stone and I want to kiss it now."

"Well," said the guide, "legend has it that if you kiss someone who has kissed the stone, you'll have the same good fortune."

"Oh, and I suppose you've kissed the stone," she scoffed.

"Well no, ma'am," said the guide, "but I've sat on it."

While visiting China, an American tourist asked his guide, "How large is the population here?"

"Around 1.5 billion," said the guide.

The American thought for a moment and said, "So, what else do you do here?"

This tourist in Israel notices that her little travel alarm needs a battery. So she looks for a watch repair shop. Since she doesn't read Hebrew she stops at a shop with clocks and watches in the window. She goes inside and hands the man her clock.

"I'm sorry. I don't repair clocks," says the man, "I am a Mohel. I do circumcisions."

"Then why all the clocks in the window?"

"And what should I have in my window?"

What's the difference between an Israeli and an Israelite?

About thirty calories.

A couple is touring the Wailing Wall in Jerusalem. They see an old Jewish man praying vigorously. When he is finished, they introduce themselves and ask about his prayers.

He says, "I have come here to pray every day for 25 years. In the morning I pray for world peace and for the brotherhood of man. I go home, have a cup of tea and I come back and pray for the eradication of illness and disease from the earth."

The couple is impressed, "How does it make you feel to come here every day for 25 years and pray for these things?"

The old man looks at them sadly and says. "Like I'm talking to a wall."

Did you hear about the highjacker who kidnapped a busload of Japanese tourists?

Police had 5000 photographs of the suspect.

Why did the tourist pass out in The Magic Kingdom?

He had Disney spells.

What do Disney World and Viagra have in common?

An hour wait for a three minute ride.

What do you call the cabs lined up at the Houston pier?

The yellow rows of taxis.

A lady goes to the San Diego Zoo to see the monkeys. It's mating season and the monkeys are hiding inside their little cave for some privacy. So the lady asks the zookeeper, "Do you think they would come out for peanuts?"

"Lady," says the zookeeper, "would you?"

A guy dies and ends up in a long line waiting for judgment. At the front of the line, some souls go to The Pearly Gates and some souls go to Satan who throws them into a fiery pit.

Every once in a while, instead of throwing them into the pit, Satan tosses one of the souls off to the side onto a small pile.

When he gets to the front of the line, the guy says, "Excuse me, Satan. I couldn't help noticing that a few of the souls get tossed into a pile instead of the fiery pit. What's the deal?"

Satan says, "Oh, those are the souls from England. They're still too wet to burn."

This couple is taking a walk around Athens one day. They're getting tired and it starts getting late, so they call a cab to take them back to their ship.

"Where are you?" asks the cab dispatcher.

Bill says, "We're on Hrissospiliotissas Way."

"Could you spell that?" says the cab driver.

Bill thinks for a minute and says, "I'll tell you what — we'll walk over to Panos Street. Meet us there."

A couple went on a Hawaiian cruise. On the four day passage, they argued back and forth about the pronunciation of the state's name.

When they got to the islands they decided to let one of the locals settle the matter. Their first day in Honolulu, they stopped to get something to eat and asked the waitress, "Before we order, could you please settle an argument for us? Real slow and real distinctly, where are we?"

The girl thought for a moment, then leaned across the counter and said, "Burrr, gerrrr, Kiiiiing."

When God created Canada, He said "I'm going to make it a land of incredible natural beauty, with snow-capped mountains, shimmering lakes and giant evergreen forests as far as the eye can see. A land rich in natural resources so all the people will prosper and be happy."

One of the angels said, "Don't you think you're being a little too generous to these people?"

"Just wait," said God. "You haven't seen the neighbors that I'm giving them."

A guy from Toronto was planning to move to Newfoundland. In order to fit in there, a friend suggested he see a neurosurgeon to have a third of his brain cut out.

After the operation, the doctor visited him in the recovery room and said, "I'm very sorry, but there was a slight problem with your surgery. Instead of cutting a third of your brain out, I accidentally cut out two-thirds."

The patient said, "Qu'est-ce que vous avez dit, monsieur?"

On a shore excursion in Australia, a Texan went to see some of the local agriculture. When his guide showed him a grove of grapefruit, the Texan laughed, "In Texas, we got lemons bigger than that!"

When his guide showed him a patch of watermelons, he laughed again, "In Texas, we got cucumbers bigger than that!"

When his guide showed him an apple orchard, the Texan laughed again, "In Texas, we got cherries bigger than that!"

Just then, a herd of kangaroos ran across the road. The Texan jumped up, startled, "What in the world was that?"

Nonchalantly, his guide answered, "Mice."

What do Australians call a boomerang that doesn't come back? A stick.

This guy goes to Tourist Information and asks, "What's the quickest way to get to the beach?"

"Are you going by car or by foot?"

"By car."

"Yes, that would be the quickest way."

A passenger wandered off during a stop in Columbia. He was hopelessly lost in the jungle for nearly a week before he ran into a local peasant walking along a dirt path.

"Thank heavens, I've met someone," he cried. "I've been lost for almost a week."

"Really?" said the peasant. "Is there a reward out for you?"

"I don't think so."

"Then I am afraid you are still lost."

On a tour of Costa Rica, the bus gets stuck . Fortunately, a local farmer passes by with his horse. The farmer ties his horse to the bumper and says, "Pull, Paco, pull!"

The horse doesn't budge.

He says, "Pull, Pedro, pull!'

The horse doesn't move.

Then he says, "Pull, Jorge, pull!

But the horse still doesn't move.

Finally he says, "Pull, Jose, pull!

The horse bolts forward and pulls the bus from the ditch.

The tour guide says, "Mucho gracious, senior."

The farmer says, "Jose and I were happy to assist you."

"Just one question," asks the guide. "Why were you calling your horse by different names?"

"I wasn't, senior," says the farmer. "You see, Jose is blind and he is also very lazy. If he thinks he is the only one pulling, he won't even try."

What do Eskimos get from sitting on the ice too long?
  Polaroids.

A Texan went on an Alaskan cruise. He was boasting to everyone about how much bigger and better everything was in Texas when an enormous iceberg floated by.

"Well," he said, " I have to admit you got bigger ice cubes."

ALASKAN GRIZZLY BEAR WARNING

While hiking in the woods, outdoorsmen should wear little bells on their clothing so as not to startle sleeping bears. It is also a good idea to watch out for fresh signs of bear activity. Hikers should recognize the difference between black bear and grizzly bear poop. Black bear poop is smaller and contains lots of berries and squirrel fur. Grizzly bear poop has little bells in it.

Two guys are out hiking when they see a bear charging at them. The first guy drops his pack and starts putting on his running shoes. The other guy says, "What are you doing? You can't outrun a bear!"

The first guy says, "I don't need to outrun the bear. I just need to outrun you."

What's the difference between tourists and mosquitoes?

Mosquitoes are only annoying in the summer.

This guy walks into a bar with his pit bull and says, "Do you serve tourists here?"

The bartender says, "Yes."

The guy says, "Great. I'll have a beer and my pit bull will have a tourist."

What do you call a tourist who speaks three languages?
   Tri-lingual.
What do you call a tourist who speaks two languages?
   Bi-lingual.
What do you call a tourist who speaks one language?
   American.

Two tourists are standing on a street corner when a cab driver pulls up and says, "Tu habla Espaniol?"
   They just stare at him.
   He says, "Sprechen si Deutsch?"
   They continue to stare.
   He says, "Parlez vous Francais?"
   Nothing.
   As he drives off, one tourist turns to the other and says, "Maybe we should learn a foreign language?"
   "What for?" says the other. "That guy knew three of them, and a fat lot of good it did him."

On a tour of a remote South Pacific island, a woman started taking pictures of some native children playing on the beach.
   When they saw what she was doing, the children began yell in protest.
   Her husband turned to her and said, "I've read that in some primitive cultures it's taboo to have your picture taken. Perhaps those children are yelling because they think you are trying to steal their souls."
   Overhearing their conversation, their guide said, "It's possible they're yelling because you forgot to remove your lens cap."

Two tourists rent a boat to go fishing. They catch a lot fish and at the end of the day, one says to the other, "We should mark this spot in case we come back someday."

The other one says, "That's a good idea! Why don't we put a big 'X' on the bottom of the boat?"

"Don't be stupid! What if we don't get the same boat?"

This tourist is sightseeing in Honduras when he sees a farmer walk by with a three-legged pig.

He says, "What's the deal with the pig?"

The farmer says, "Oh senor, that is the best pig in the whole world. He saved my life."

"He saved your life?"

"Yes," said the farmer, "there was a big fire in my village and I was trapped inside my barn. No one noticed because they were too busy fighting the flames. But the pig, he noticed. He ran into the barn after me and dragged me to safety."

"That's an amazing story," said the tourist, "but why does the pig only have three legs."

"Well, senor, a pig that good, you can't eat all at once."

Why didn't grandpa get upset when the customs officials went through his luggage at the border?

Because they found his glasses he lost two weeks earlier.

A guy goes into a souvenir shop. He points to a clay pot and says, "What's that?"

The shopkeeper says, "It's Brazilian."

The guy says, "Wow, that's a lot."

After wandering all day, the tour group was hopelessly lost in the jungle. When the tour guide finally admitted he had no idea how to get back to the ship, one of the angry hikers said, "How could this happen? I thought you were the best guide in Costa Rica!"

"I am," replied the guide, "but I think we're in Honduras now."

This old guy rents a moped to go sightseeing. He's sitting at a stop light when a young guy in a Ferrari pulls up. The old guy says, "That's one heck of a car. Do you mind if I look around inside?"

The young guy says okay. So the old man sticks his head in and looks around, " I bet it goes pretty fast, hunh?"

"It sure does," says the young guy, and when the light turns green, he revs the engine and races away.

A few minutes later, he notices the moped is right behind him. He floors the accelerator, but the moped is still right on his tail. No matter how fast he goes, he can't lose him.

Finally, he puts on the brakes and when he stops, the moped slams into the back his car.

The driver jumps out of his car and says, "Mister, are you okay? Is there anything I can do?"

The old guy looks up and says, "Yeah, could you unhook my suspenders from your rear view mirror?"

About The Author

Elliot Maxx has been a popular comedian on cruise ships and in nightclubs for many years.

He has appeared on Showtime, MTV and Comedy Central, and shared the concert stage with such legendary artists as Tony Bennett, Ray Charles and Roy Orbison.

Elliot makes his home in Seattle along with his wife, three kids, and their menagerie of pets.

He recently released his first album, entitled, "Songs That Annoy My Wife."

If you'd like to share your favorite joke, please email: ELLIOTMAXX@MSN.COM